I0220793

Broken Hearts in a Broken World

by

Gerard M. Verschuuren

ENROUTE
Make the time

En Route Books and Media, LLC
5705 Rhodes Avenue
St. Louis, MO 63109

Cover credit: TJ Burdick

LCCN: 2018967673

Copyright © 2018 Gerard M. Verschuuren
All rights reserved.

ISBN-13: 978-1-950108-01-5
ISBN-10: 1-950108-01-5

Table of Contents

Preface

Broken! It's one of those words that doesn't bring a lot of joy. Who wants to be broken? Bones are broken, promises are broken, expectations are broken, homes are broken, hearts are broken. As a matter of fact, our lives are full of brokenness.

Brokenness has become endemic in our days. In poll after poll, the vast majority of respondents say that our country is fundamentally broken. Our political system is broken. Our economy is broken. And our very society, the way we live together, our values, our priorities, all of them are broken. Although the question doesn't come up in too many polls, I bet most people—if they are honest with themselves—would admit that they themselves are broken, too. How can we live with so much brokenness without becoming bitter?

For Christians, however, the brokenness of the world and their own brokenness should not come as breaking news. Reaching all the way back to the beginnings of our Judeo-Christian tradition, there has been a clear understanding that creation, the entire world, is broken. As a matter of fact, there seems to be brokenness all over. In this book, we will see how much brokenness is around us: how broken our generation is (Chapter 1), how broken our world is (Chapter 2), how broken our families are (Chapter 3), how broken our hearts are (Chapter 4), and how broken our souls are (Chapter 5).

That must make for a gloomy book, you might think. But that's jumping to conclusions too fast. Not only are there cures for brokenness, but there is even glory in brokenness. For Christians, brokenness and the healing of brokenness are at the very heart of the Christian faith. Christians believe that God became a human being in Jesus, who suffered and died on the Cross. He came to be among the broken-hearted in a broken world to experience and heal our brokenness. Jesus came into the flesh—and with that flesh comes suffering and brokenness. If Jesus is broken, then God in fact knows brokenness in flesh and blood. That's a very painful, yet comforting thought behind this book.

1. A Broken Generation

An X-Ray of a Broken Generation

There were times that generations did not change much. Each new generation was basically a copy of the previous generation. But today that does no longer seem to be the case. The "new" generation is different from the "older" generation, both in the eyes of the older generation and in the eyes of the new generation. They both speak of a "generation gap" that separates them, and with that seems to come the notion of a "broken" generation, especially seen from the other side of the gap.

Is there really such a gap? Probably both sides do agree that there is not as much communality between the old and new generation as there used to be. It is often very hard for a family to even enjoy major celebrations such as Christmas and Thanksgiving Day together without fights erupting over religion, politics, and traditions. Sports might be the exception, but lately, even there, divisive politics is creeping in as well.

There is hardly any doubt about the fact that our society is changing in a way that affects both sides of the generation gap, but in particular the new generation. Statistics tell us that family life—that is to say, the married two-parent family—is going downhill rapidly. Among blacks, the married two-parent family has largely vanished, and among non-blacks it is moving swiftly in the same direction. The time is coming, if it hasn't already arrived, when the typical boy or girl will grow up without two married parents in the home. And even if a couple is married, pets are preferred over children.

These are some general observations about the new generation. As a matter of fact, it is hard to not fall into grossly generalized platitudes about the new generation. But perhaps the following scene could be a starter. The family is sitting together at the dining table. First of all, that may not happen too often nowadays, as everyone, young and old, is in for a quick meal on their way to a next appointment. But let's assume it does happen. What is taking place then and there? Perhaps the children are all staring at their Smartphone, texting on their iPad, talking on their cellphone, or playing with any of their other latest gadgets. But let's assume there is a moment of conversation. It could be about anything, but most likely about some contentious issue that divides the family. And if the parents do ask their children how school was—which they, hopefully, do often—they may be told the answer can be found on their blog. I know this picture is extreme, but it does convey some basic truth. The so-called generation gap spans all across the family table.

I like to focus in this section on the latest generation: In what sense could this be a broken generation? Which calls for a "diagnosis." And later, in the "cure" section, we should find out what the previous generation could possibly do better, or should have done better.

What do we mean when we speak of "the new generation"? They have been named and distinguished in many different ways. If you take the dates with a grain of salt, there is a generation of "Baby-Boomers," born between 1946 and 1964, a generation of "Gen-X," born between 1965 and 1979, a generation of "Millennials," born between 1980 and 2000, and then there is the latest generation of "iGen," born after 2000. They all differ from each other in some way, but what unites them is that they seem to be rather different from the "older" generation that was born around the end of World War II.

So the new generation is in fact a collective term for several new generations. Let's not forget that, at one point, everyone belonged to the "new" generation. Having said that, however, the new generation does differ from older generations in various ways—at least in political, social, moral, and religious terms. These different ways are probably closely connected, but let's discuss them separately.

Let's start with the *political* differences. We could be very extensive on this issue, but a short generalization might suffice. Throughout the 1980s and 90s, younger and older adults voted in largely similar ways, with a majority of each supporting the winner in every presidential election. Sometime around 2004, though, older voters began moving right, while younger voters shifted left. Since then, polls suggest that one candidate will win a landslide among the 65+ crowd and that the other candidate will do likewise among those under 40.

Beyond political parties, the two have different views on many of the biggest questions concerning the country. The young not only favor gay marriage and school funding more strongly, but they are also notably less religious, more positive toward immigrants, less hostile to Social Security cuts and military cuts, and more optimistic about the country's future. Forgive me for another generalization, but the new generation somehow lives in a "global" world and culture that potentially stretches over the entire globe. All of them wear the same kind of jeans, watch the same kind of videos, use the same social media. Somehow, what was once considered American culture has become an export culture that tries to infiltrate the entire world. The new generation considers itself part of that "global" world.

Besides, there is this optimistic idea that anything "new under the sun" is better than what we had before because many believe that human society is in constant progress, up the ladder of evolution, on a journey to a better and better future, especially in a political way. It's hard to believe, though, that this is true. We have indeed witnessed many new discoveries, improvements, and technologies, but they all come with serious "side-effects." So progress seems to always come at a cost—with some regress at the same time.

When we turn to the *social* aspect of the generation gap, what strikes many of us most is the size of families, especially the number of children. First, there is the idea that we should have only a few of them, if we want any at all: small families are in, large families are out. Much of America, especially liberal America, was shocked, when at the death of Justice Antonin Scalia in early 2016, we heard that he and his wife were the parents of nine children. By present-day standards, that's too many—far too many, they said. Is it that Americans, by and large, don't care about children? But this is obviously not true, given the vast amount of energy and money parents spend to make sure that their children are well-fed, well-clothed, well-housed, and well-educated. But we must add, all of that is only material care. At a deeper level, more is going on.

Second, there is the fact that more and more families are no longer families in the traditional sense. The traditional family seems to have become a thing of the past. Nowadays it's perfectly fine to have divorced parents. Since divorce was made easier by civil law, the number of divorces has been on the rise. It used to be rather common for parents to have four or more children; nowadays, it is rather common for children to have four or more parents.

Third, nowadays it's also perfectly fine to be an unmarried mother. As for the father, not only is there no longer a social duty to marry the mother, but there is no social duty even to cohabit with her on a permanent basis. We should ask ourselves the question of what does the fact that 68% of African-American babies are born out of wedlock suggest. In the white community, the figure is now 22%, and rapidly growing. But again, not only does this create a broken new generation, it is also the result of a broken preceding generation. Let's not forget that generations are "generated" by generations before them. Without a preceding generation, we would not have a new generation.

No matter how, we ended up with a fatherless generation. The children of that generation do have two parents—that's a biological necessity—but no fathers. They have no one who claimed authority when they were growing up. As adult authority disintegrates, the new generation "listens" to peers—to what their peers feel, think, believe, and do. Because their fathers failed them, they traded the father's authority in for the clout of peers. Psychologists tell us that we drifted from a guilt culture to a shame culture, from feeling *guilt* about not living up to expectations of one's parents to feeling *shame* from not keeping in line with one's little group of peers. That's how the social aspect of the generation gap has dramatically changed.

Not only is there a political and social aspect to the generation gap, but also a *moral* one. In a nutshell, recent generations have gone through a sexual revolution, which was meant to "liberate" men and women from any stifling morality, from what is now considered as antiquated traditions and moral codes. Because the sexual revolution identifies love with sex, sex has taken over. The use of artificial contraceptives is one of the main driving forces behind the current "sexual revolution" because it allows sex at any time with anyone anywhere without any "risk" of pregnancy. In this view, sex is for fun, not for babies. However, if sex for fun by mistake does lead to babies, we need to prevent that, which in turn leads to abortion, portrayed now as simple as the removal of an appendix. In other words, abortion is, in Peter Kreeft's words, "backup birth control, and birth control is the demand to have sex without having babies."

The new generation sees abortion as a tool to liberate women. However, contrary to popular opinion, abortion hurts women. The *Medical Science Monitor* published alarming data in 2003 and 2004. Here are some results. Women have a 65% higher risk of clinical depression following abortion compared to childbirth. Abortion increases a woman's risk of future miscarriages by 60%. Suicide rates among women who had abortions are six times higher than those who gave birth. Their death rates from various causes after abortion are 3.5 times higher than after giving birth. Based on these figures, we could say that abortion is more of a "nightmare" than a "healthy choice." Some 60% of women surveyed after abortion responded, "Part of me died." This doesn't quite sound like the removal of an appendix.

On the other hand, if a child does get born and become part

of a new generation, we are supposed to give it a freedom similar to the freedom women demand for themselves. This is the freedom of who they want to be. There are "gender ideologists" who want us to believe that we are not born as "F" or "M" but "X," so that we can then later decide, in all freedom, whether we want to be "F," "M," or anything in between. This "gender ideology" obviously denies a person's identity as a man or a woman. Your sex is supposedly no longer something you were born with, when the doctor said "It's a boy," or "It's a girl." Gender is supposedly something we choose ourselves. If John says he is a woman, then John is a woman—that is a matter of his or her right.

In the new generation, gender-identity basically depends on how children want to define "their sexual reality." They are who they say they are, if they say so. This may also make some people decide to undergo sex-change surgery because they feel that their soul is "trapped" in the body of the wrong sex. What previous generations took for granted—that words such as *man, woman, mother,* and *father* name natural realities as well as social roles—is now increasingly regarded as obsolete because some trend-makers decided to redefine "gender" as referring to *the sex with which a person identifies*. If a male identifies with the female sex, they say, that must be his, or now her, "real" sex, so doctors must make it come true. So, we end up with a generation of males, females, *and* everything in-between.

As a consequence, the new generation lives in a murky world of moral confusion. What ought to be sexual identity was turned into gender identity, what ought to be marriage is replaced by "relationship," what ought to be courtship is replaced by "consensual sexual intercourse," and what ought to be innocent ways for young people to get to know one another is replaced by basically nothing at all. What has this led to? At campuses, for instance, where vice reigns over virtues, many women flock to the safe space of a "women's studies" program, and many men find themselves caught in the grip of a "rape culture." That's probably not the outcome we had hoped for, but it is in line with what the sexual revolution had started.

Not only is there a political, social, and moral aspect to the generation gap, but also a *religious* one. The old generation considers the celebration of Thanksgiving Day a precious old tradition. The new generation celebrates Black Friday instead as a tradition worth keeping. And they may wish you "Happy Turkey Day" instead of "Happy Thanksgiving Day." But the differences go much deeper than these superficial differences.

The new generation deems religion to be a matter of mere personal views, feelings, sentiments, and opinions. However, something declared as a "feeling" or a "sentiment" cannot be "disputed" as being true or false. Any discussion about it has become impossible. "About taste, there is no dispute," as the old Latin adage goes. If "feeling" is the category under which we find out about things, we can have no argument for or against it. "Feelings" as such are absolute—either we have them, or we do not. Nevertheless, a generation in which only "feelings" seem to count presumes at least one truth: the truth of the statement that only feelings, not truths, exist and count. Question that statement and the world of the primacy of feelings collapses.

As a result, the new generation mostly rejects the truth of religion. The religious concerns, questions, and answers of previous generations—including those of their parents—have lost their meaning for many of the new generation. If there is anything worthwhile in life, then it must be here and now. It all depends on the present, without a past and a future. What tomorrow brings depends on what makes sense to us today—that is, the people you meet and the ideas you hear. And it also depends on what is not local but rather "global"—on what we find in other cultures and religions, anywhere on earth.

This makes for a generation that is no longer religious. Research tells us that the religiously unaffiliated population is typically younger, predominately male, with 35% between the ages of 18 and 29, whereas only 8% of religiously unaffiliated individuals are 65 and older (but the numbers change quickly). Some of these people call themselves "nones." They are not affiliated with any "brand-name" religion and believe nothing religious in particular. Others call themselves "spiritual," which means that they reject what they call "traditional or organized religion." Their spirituality is basically an amalgam of elements such as tai chi, reiki, and yoga, which they have lumped together from various sources based on their own liking.

So where does all of this leave us in the "battle" of the generations? There is this story that a college freshman attending a football game tried to explain to a veteran sitting next to him why it was impossible for the older generation to understand his own generation. "You grew up in a different world," the student said, loud enough for those nearby to hear. "The young people of today grew up with television, jet planes, man walking on the moon, spaceships visiting Mars. We have nuclear energy, electric and hydrogen cars, computers with light-speed processing. And...," pausing to take another sip of his beer. The veteran took advantage of the break in the student's litany and said, "You're right, son. We didn't have those things when we were young, so we invented them for you. Now, you, what are you doing for the next generation?"

But I also need to stress again that we cannot make sweeping statements about something as diverse as a generation. Just think of the fact that pro-life marches have a growing number of young participants; there are countless youth-oriented and even youth-organized events surrounding the March for Life. Or take the controversial play *The Vagina Monologues*. The play delves into consensual and nonconsensual sexual experiences, genital mutilation, direct and indirect experiences with reproduction, sex, and several other topics seen through the eyes of women with various ages, races, sexualities, and other differences. It seems to be a prefect portrayal of what the new generation is like. But as Naomi Schaefer Riley noted in the *Wall Street Journal* about events in 2008 at Notre Dame University: "About thirty students walked out of *The Vagina Monologues* in protest after the first scene. And people familiar with the university are not surprised that it was the kids, not the grownups, who registered the strongest objections." Although it is true that half of all the Catholic children baptized or confirmed these last thirty years no longer participate in the life of the Church, this event of 2008 at Notre Dame University is just an example to show us it is never right to praise or condemn an entire generation. Although the number of "nones" is rising, we also see an increase of countercultural communities on campuses of universities. Didn't we see the rise of the John-Paul-II-Generation not too long ago? That's the other side of the story.

When talking about a "generation gap," there is this common conception that the future lies with the young. However, by giving the new generation too much honor—actually overweight—we don't give them the honor they do deserve. Being young, in and of itself, doesn't call for condemnation, but equally not for glorification. One is as little justified as the other. The newer and the older generation just need one another. Without listening to the older generation, young people become conceited; without listening to the younger generation, old people turn antiquated. You, generations, please listen to each other, for God's sake!

Yet, it is always tempting, especially for the older generation, to call the new generation the broken generation. They tend to live with the nostalgia of "the good old days." In Roman times, a person who thought that way was called "a praiser of past times" [*laudator temporis acti*]. Thinking that the past is always better than the present is as one-sided as the thought that the new is always better than the old. We need to realize that the new generation did not come out of the blue, but instead came forth from the previous generation—the generation of their parents, that is. It's clear that both sides of the generation gap—if there is such a thing—are in trouble. Didn't the older generation "generate" the new generation? So it is not fair to say that the new generation is broken, for apparently the older generation must be broken as well since it partly caused the brokenness of the new generation. Broken generations breed broken generations.

In other words, it's not quite clear who in fact represents the broken generation. Is it the older, parent generation, thinking they have failed to bring up their children the way they had hoped for? Or is it the new generation, the children generation, who think their parents have failed in giving them what they had dreamed of? Or is it the parent generation, who feels disconnected from their children? Or is it perhaps the new generation of those who think they never had the parents they should have had?

It's probably all of the above. It's always convenient to blame the generation on the other side of the “gap.” It’s hard to believe that one generation is better than the other. If you think that the new generation is the broken one, you must admit that they could not be what they are without the previous generation. If you believe the old generation is the broken one, you can’t forget that the new generation arose from the old generation and therefore must be broken, too.

But there is another dimension to this. It’s rather simplistic to blame only the older generation when we see something wrong with the new generation. The previous generation is not the only factor determining how the next generation comes along. There is also the environment in which the new generation grows up. This environment has changed quite a bit in recent years. There are strong currents now of ideas that seem to counteract what older generations had cherished. Two in particular are relativism and secularism.

These new ideas make it much harder to bring up a generation that is still in line with what was previously believed, practiced, and hoped for. Media and academia are the strong motors of these ideas. They seem to have joined forces to destruct the pillars of previous generations. Together, they are so powerful and widespread that it is hard to swim against the current. First of all, they make us believe there is no longer absolute truth: Whatever is true for me may be false for you; whatever is right for me may be wrong for someone else. This idea belies the centuries-old belief—one of the pillars of previous generations—that truth is truth, even if you do not accept it; and untruth is untruth, even if you claim it. Truth is truth—for everyone, anywhere, at any time. If the world is round, then someone’s opposing opinion won’t make it flat. To think differently is called relativism.

However, the problem for relativism is that it contradicts

itself. Relativists can only avoid contradiction by putting a restriction on the original claim: all truths are relative except the one of relativism. But if they do so, they should ask themselves what entitles someone to make this exception. Apparently, this position leaves us with at least one objective truth—the objective truth of relativism itself. Why not more then? The problem with a claim like "There is no such a thing as objective truth" is that it claims to be objectively true. We cannot make such a sweeping assertion without also asserting, implicitly, that there is such a thing as objective truth after all.

Denying that there is objective truth means you are insisting in your denial that what you say is objectively true—which cannot be true by its own verdict. Relativism cannot protect itself from its own contradiction. In the meantime, relativism has made us lose respect for the truth, so now the door is wide open to "fake news." Truth is not something we create or invent, but something we try to "capture." Ironically, a frequently used expression in the mouth of relativists is the exclamation "absolutely" in almost every statement they utter. When questioned whether their "fake news" is true, relativists tend to shout, "Absolutely!"

Then there is a second pillar of previous generations that these joined forces want to attack. They try to make us believe that society should not only enjoy freedom *of* religion—instead of one religion enforced by the State—but also freedom *from* religion. That's called secularism. It has an anti-religious overtone—a vision of a State as devoid of religion, instead of separated from religion. It seeks to eliminate religion, or at the very least to privatize and thus marginalize it. In doing so, secularism reveals itself as totalitarian, for it allows no room in the public square for anything but itself. Secularists want only their views and values to be taught and allowed in public life. Unquestionably, it is hard for any generation to swim against these strong tides of relativism and secularism, especially so for the youngest generation. It's one, yet important, reason why the new generation is broken.

This does not alter the fact, though, that the environment is still to a large extent behind the creation of previous generations as well. So we cannot really find out why the new generation is broken if we don't address also the question of why the old generation was so broken that they did not prevent their children from becoming another broken generation. Members of broken generations "breed" more broken generations. What is it then that they did not give the younger generation? Probably the shortest, but also too general, answer is: They didn't give them an *identity* because they themselves did not have an identity. They actually have lost confidence in the moral and religious values they received themselves, so they have become estranged from the values that inspired them in the past.

A Cure for a Broken Generation?

Is there a cure for broken generations? When I speak of "a cure," I am not claiming that the therapy suggested here would be the best therapy. You might even wonder whether there is actually any cure that will heal a broken generation. And if there is one, it will most likely not work automatically or automagically. It calls for hard work. It is the hard work of giving broken generations back their *identity*. So let's find out how this might be done.

How do you get or give an identity? It is probably a gradual and long process. We can see what happens to children who were given complete freedom instead of an identity. They were never disciplined and never heard "no" in their upbringing. When they don't get in the store what they want, they go into a tantrum—and usually that changes any initial "no" into another "yes." Of course, we can't blame the children—they took on what their parents taught them, or rather did *not* teach them. Their parents let them choose whatever they wanted: freedom instead of identity. They tell their little ones to choose in the grocery store whatever they want, although those toddlers have no idea at that age of what the difference is between all the items displayed or what is best for them. In a similar way, they let their kids choose which elementary school they like best. They let them choose what they would like to learn. They let them decide later which religion they want. In the meantime, they let them live in a complete vacuum of nothingness. The underlying misconception is that it is better to start from scratch than on a foundation of experience, common sense, and tradition, which makes many of us believe that each new generation should literally start anew, with no roots and no history—that is, with no identity. How can you choose if you don't know where to begin and what to go by?

Why is identity so vital for any generation, old or new? Usually we speak of "identity" in relationship to individuals, but it can also be applied to a group of individuals, including an entire generation. In reference to individuals, identity is usually understood as bodily identity. We tend to locate our identity in our bodies. What do I mean by that?

Each person starts his or her life as a fertilized egg cell outfitted with its own, "personal," human chromosomes and human DNA. What remains the same during the entire process of adding, replacing, and losing cells during further development is the person's bodily identity. Humans have the capacity to undergo biological change without losing their identity. Although our bodies change constantly, we ourselves do not—that is, our personal identity remains the same. No matter whether cells in my body keep being replaced, the identity of my body stays the same. About 98 percent of the atoms of the adult human body, including those found in the brain and nervous system, are replaced in about every two years.

From conception on, we are persons with either a male or a female identity of the body, and nothing can change that fact—which is not to say that we may still be more or less feminine or masculine in our behavior. A person's body is a fundamental indication of what sex he or she belongs to. It is a physical, anatomical, genetic, and empirically verifiable reality that does not change simply because our beliefs or desires do. One can mutilate one's genitals, but one cannot change one's sex. One can change what genitalia and gonads one was born with, but not one's sex. You cannot "re-invent" yourself that way, because you never "invented" yourself to begin with. You received an identity during conception.

But in addition to the identity of the body, there is also an identity of the *soul*. What does the identity of the soul stand for? It means that you have boundaries and continuity in what you think and do—that you have identity beyond the here-and-now, regardless of space and time. When people lose the identity of their souls, they live exclusively in the here-and-now and are fully at the mercy of the here-and-now, drifting on the waves of their surroundings. (More on the soul in Chapter 5.)

That's basically what has happened to a broken generation lacking an identity. Its members live solely in the here-and-now. Living exclusively in the *now* means having no roots in the past and no more continuity, making people prisoners of the now, without any connections with the past. They have lost a sense of continuity and just lead a life without history. And living in the *here* means having no more boundaries and being completely at the mercy of whatever surrounds them.

Continuity protects us from the randomness of the "now." It protects our identity from what is disruptive to what is already there from the past. Boundaries protect us from the randomness of the "here." They protect our identity from disruptions by what is contrary to what we have already acquired, so that we are not "all over the place." In other words, it is essential for the identity of our souls that we live not merely in the here-and-now, tossed around by whatever hits us here and now. Otherwise, we live our lives without any roots and without any compass—that is, without any identity. We feel lost on the waves of life. We have become persons living the life of wanderers. Wanderers have no higher purpose in life than mere survival.

As a consequence of a disrupted identity, the link with previous generations has been broken, which makes for a wounded and broken generation that has no links, or only broken links, with the past. There is no longer *truth* handed down from generation to generation. For the new generation, truth is something that we are supposed to get from our peers, from our little in-group, from the city or state we happen to live in, from the time period we happen to be in—or it's merely something we have come up with on our own. This concept of truth is what we called earlier *relativism*, entirely centering on the here-and-now, and no longer transcending the here-and-now. However, the identity of the soul should not be at the mercy of a specific time period or a specific locality. It should not be corrupted and invaded by whatever we take on from our surroundings. Instead it should be based on who we really are—based on truth, rather than feelings, emotions, or opinions. Be yourself—not anyone else.

What is wrong with feelings? Feelings can be very deceiving—they can help us or they can damage us. Unfortunately, feelings can also mislead us. The whole modern therapeutic industry is built on that fact. A person suffering from depression or anxiety or any other troubling emotions should never just be told to trust those feelings. Perhaps we can find out what caused them or how we can cure them. But feelings as such need something else, a standard outside of them, to tell us precisely how, and how much, to trust them—or not. As such, they can either improve or harm who we are.

Where do we develop the identity of the soul? The shortest answer is: in the family—more in particular in the "nuclear" family of parents and children, and to a smaller degree in the "extended" family of aunts, uncles, grandparents, and other relatives. Whereas the identity of the body is partly rooted in our DNA, the identity of the soul has different roots which grow and develop during our upbringing. In the nuclear family, truth is handed down from the generation of parents to the generation of children. In the nuclear family, we learn how to deal with our feelings. We need to train emotions. We need to nurture those emotions that are in harmony with reality and truth. The alternative is to live with psychological turmoil, which leads to drug and alcohol abuse, violence, and social chaos. It's only after others, starting with parents and family, have helped us to see things in truth. It's only after we have made serious efforts on our own to be formed by perennial wisdom that we know how and when and why to "trust our feelings," so they can become part of our roots.

It should not surprise us then that especially people who have no roots often take on an endless search of past generations, delving into their "family tree" through the internet, sometimes even with the help of some DNA-kit. It's like a frantic search for broken links. It used to be tradition to give newborns a first name coming from a parent or grandparent, or of a favorite saint, but nowadays parents like to come up with their own newly invented names, preferably spelled in a strange way—which makes for another broken link with previous generations. Names used to tell you something about where you came from and whom you were named after. Now they often point to nowhere.

Nowadays, odd names are given to children to express their individuality, but that does certainly not enhance their identity. It only started a ridiculous-name craze. More than 300 people, most of them girls, were named "Abcde," pronounced ab-si-dee. Some parents chose to reverse names for fun to something like "Semaj," which made the list of top 1,000 names for boys in 1999. Even a reasonable name like "Tamara," is tricky because peers may change it into "Tomorrow." It is obvious that this name craze has dramatically reduced traditional names such as "Mary," which held the #1 spot until 1961; in 2011 it had dropped to the 112th spot in popularity. All of this was done in the name of individuality, but certainly not in the name of identity. However, the family is not a laboratory for experimentation.

But the truth remains that the generation of the parents is vital to hand down the truths they had received themselves. That's why the Fourth Commandment says, "Honor your father and your mother." Parents are our lifeline, not only to previous generations, but ultimately to God. They were—or at least should be—the first ones to tell us about God and about all we know about him. The Catechism of the Catholic Church (2197) stresses this very clearly: "[W]e should honor our parents to whom we owe life and who have handed on to us the knowledge of God." In short, "the family is the original cell of social life... an initiation into life in society" (CCC 2207). Since parents are our lifeline to God, loving them is an expression of our loving God. So through them, we love the One our parents gave to us.

What parents hand on to their children is the rich tradition of their religion, among many other truths of life. Tradition means literally: something we "pass or hand on." If you want to give up traditions, customs, and insights that were tested through many generations, you need very convincing reasons to do so. Unfortunately, our culture doesn't appreciate what has been handed down because it is often considered second-hand. Indeed, the material things that we pass on usually deteriorate with age. But the tradition that the Fourth Commandment refers to doesn't deteriorate; it is more like gold that doesn't tarnish; it is definitely first-hand—directly from God. It usually comes to us through our parents. Children not only inherit the genetic traits of their parents, but they also receive a family history, an ethnic culture, and a religious heritage.

Unfortunately, some parents failed in their mission because they never passed on much of God's truths; but fortunately, God's reliance on parents is a relative one, and not a definite one. And then there are parents who think they failed because their children didn't accept the "tradition" they handed on to them. There may be many reasons for this. Sometimes, evil forces from outside the family took over. Sometimes, parents just failed to be there for their kids—just too busy with their own problems. At times, the black shadows of their views darkened the lives of their children. At other times, they stood in someone else's way. So children may not always be able to respect their parents, but they are still asked to *honor* them by loving them, even though they may have failed in their "mission." Honoring your parents means to give them the weight they have received from God; not the weight they have given themselves!

Parents are supposed to help their children to develop their own identity. If you know your identity, you know who you are. In the musical *Fiddler on the Roof*, this is famously called "tradition." As Tevye says, "Because of our traditions, we've kept our balance for many, many years.... Because of our traditions, everyone knows who he is and what God expects him to do." Parents who know who they are, are probably more likely to raise children who also know who they are. But that is exactly where broken generations come in. Generations become broken when they have lost the identity of the soul or have never received any because parents did not give them the roots and boundaries we all need to develop properly.

Some might object that children should develop their own identity. "Let them find their own identity," is the new mantra. But how can you find your own identity if you have no identity to begin with? Nowadays, we have been brainwashed by the idea that we start from nothing and from there on decide what we want to be. However, if you are no-one, it is very hard to become some-one. Nothing comes from nothing, as the saying goes. The one thing we know about "nothing" is that it's literally nothing. No wonder many end up completely confused, twisted, and mixed-up. They are empty vessels that were randomly filled with anything whatsoever. They no longer know who they are.

Being mixed-up by lack of identity starts already at a very basic level. We said earlier that we are born as boy or girl, man or woman—which is the identity of our bodies. But does this mean that parents should give us the choice as to how we develop this identity in the soul, so we can then later decide whether we want to be "F" or "M" or anything in-between. The problem is, though, that persons whose biological identity is male cannot have a female gender identity; if they think they do, it is only in their minds as an imitation of the other sex, for whatever reason. Sexual orientation is not a social construction but a biological one that is essential to our identity. Our bodies contain a self-sufficient digestive or respiratory system, but it only contains half of a reproductive system and must be paired with a half-system belonging to a person of the opposite sex in order to carry out its function. These are undeniable biological facts. They are an essential part of our identity.

Unfortunately, "gender ideologists" want us to believe that not only gender is a *social* construction, but also sex. So they tell us it is politically incorrect to bring up boys as boys and girls as girls. However, the "typical" boy, with his more advanced spatial skills, may well prefer activities like climbing, or pushing trucks around—all of which further sharpen his visual-spatial skills. The "typical" girl, by contrast, may gravitate more toward games with dolls and siblings, which further reinforce her verbal and social skills. On the other hand, this does not mean there aren't wonderful opportunities to compensate for the different "tendencies" of boys and girls. But it is nonsense to say that dolls should be given to boys also for the reason that being a boy is supposedly a merely social construction. That is probably not helping their identity; we should rather confirm their given sexual identity. The point is not to discourage children from sex-typical play, but we may want to supplement those activities with experiences that encourage the development of a wider range of capabilities, without confusing them.

Although René Descartes made us believe that the soul is "trapped" in the body, body and soul are in fact intricately connected. There is no such thing as a female soul trapped in a male body, or reversed. Once we disconnect the soul from the body, we actually create an identity crisis. This makes an entirely isolated soul decide on its own what the body should be, male or female or whatever. Some people decide to even undergo sex-change surgery because they feel this "entrapment" of their soul in the body of the opposite sex. All of a sudden, some medical and psychological professionals have created, out of thin air, a "disorder" over we supposedly have no further control. No wonder the actual consequences are quite disastrous.

A recent report by the psychiatrists Lawrence Mayer and Paul McHugh of Johns Hopkins Medical School, based on nearly 200 peer-reviewed studies of sexual orientation and gender identity, discloses some striking information. First, only a minority of children who express gender-atypical thoughts or behavior will continue to do so into adolescence or adulthood. Second, among transgender individuals, 41% have attempted suicide, whereas only 4.6% of the overall U.S. population reports "a lifetime suicide attempt." So the hypothesis of "social stress" as an explanation has so far not been corroborated. Third, one hospital's practice of surgically removing the poorly-developed genitalia of male infants and giving them female genitalia showed that, years later, most of the subjects still identified as male, although their parents had been directed to raise the boys as girls.

What we should conclude from this is the important role of parents to help their children develop the right identity—and sexual identity is only one part of it. Because of an increasing number of broken families and same-sex parents, the right parent may not be available for the child to identify with, and therefore its gender may not have a chance to line up with the appropriate sex. This may have quite an impact on the new generation and may easily lead to an identity crisis.

Interestingly enough, we live in a time and a generation where we determine our own identity—not as something given to us, but as something claimed by us. However, we are "contingent" beings, which means we are unable to keep ourselves in existence. As a consequence, we don't have sufficient knowledge to self-identify since we are a mystery even to ourselves. So, in order to know who we are, we must seek enlightenment from God—and not from what the philosopher Charles Taylor calls the "sovereign self." Only God can self-identify because he relies or depends on nothing to be himself. Ironically, at a time when everyone wants the power to self-identify, we rob this ability from God. God is the only being who could realistically and accurately "self-identify."

This takes us to another serious problem of broken generations: the broken family (more on this later in Chapter 3). Children need the stable, identity-forming environment of the nuclear family. If they do not grow in this environment, they run a serious risk of being wounded or crippled in their identity for the rest of their lives. Because they may not know who their father is—caused by divorce or as a result of artificial insemination—they may not even know themselves. In cases like this, the brokenness of the new generation is obviously caused by the brokenness of the previous generation. The identity of the new generation rests squarely on the foundation of the nuclear family. More and more members of the new generation are born out of wedlock. One of two marriages is going to end in divorce. Dr. Rebecca Peck, MD, a family practice physician, says in no uncertain terms:

> *The saddest women I see in medical practice are single women, depressed and exhausted from trying to work and fulfill the role of mother and father. Children are neglected. Poverty and violence are increasing. The traditional family is becoming a thing of the past.*

Because of all that was broken in the previous generation, this very brokenness has been handed down to the new generation. Because there is no longer continuity, people with a broken identity take on whatever strikes them at the here-and-now—that is, any kind of ideology, any kind of conviction, any kind of tradition, any kind of life style, any kind of religion or spirituality. They actually claim we should experiment which each one of them, just to become what they call "a more diverse person," instead of a more integrated person with an identity. They are told that different ideas, convictions, and lifestyles should be embraced to discover something new.

But how do we tell people without roots that not everything different or new is of the same quality? And something similar holds for people who don't have the boundaries needed to keep their identity intact. It is hard to tell this to a generation of people who have no more boundaries. They no longer know what to believe, whom to trust, what to pursue. The outcome is predictable: Why not try then something they have never tried before? And so they do, through mass media, social media, and the internet—which makes them even more twisted and confused. They become actually aimless and rudderless.

It may sound strange at first sight, but honoring the tradition of the older generation is not a matter of nostalgia; instead it provides the next generation a foundation for renewal and innovation—provided the older generation still has a foundation. The nuclear family creates the conditions in which the new generation can feel secure to develop its own identity. Therefore, the older generation must assume responsibility to pass on its cultural, intellectual, and religious legacy. A generation that rejects this responsibility raises children that lack the values that inspired others in the past. It is actually impossible to engage with the future unless people draw on the experience of past generations.

It is clear, we have to give a broken generation its identity back—that means boundaries and continuity. Well, that is easier said than done, but how do you do such a thing? The most important tool, or therapy, is probably a restoration of the nuclear family. We have to make the family as healthy as possible again, for that's where the new generation is born. If one or both of the parents are absent, the children's identity is in danger. They are sent into the world without knowing who they are. They are all over the place, but never "at home." This even shows in the diminishing interaction between people on the streets of our cities. It makes them feel cut off from the human family at large. Countless people commit suicide because there is nobody waiting for them, for there is no reason to live if there is nobody to live for. They never had a real "home."

Obviously, it's vital for future generations that we give them back the identity of their souls, which starts at home! Even a fatherless generation is still looking for someone who gives them an identity and thus liberates them from the vicious circle of immediate needs that ask for immediate satisfaction. No wonder then so many people are emotionally starved. Instead of providing drugs, we should be giving hugs. Instead of passing out baskets of condoms, we should hand out valentines. Perhaps many adults of the older generation are as much in need of "sex education" as the younger generation so as to learn that love is more than sex. The best therapy for a broken generation begins with reinstating and reinforcing the nuclear family. (More on the family in Chapter 3.)

This may require lots of self-giving. Self-giving is not so much a matter of nice, warm feelings, but of self-giving actions. In a marriage, the romantic feelings of love may disappear at times, but a deep sense of commitment should remain steering daily actions in good days as well as bad days. Even Jesus himself, when he gave of himself in suffering and death, did not do so with positive feelings, but it was his ultimate act of self-giving. In daily life, we often have to "give in," but the secret is to transform "giving in" to "giving"—like the husband who says to his wife, "For you, I will do it," with or without any warm feelings. This is like saying, "I will do it, not because I feel like it, but because I want to do it for you." "To feel" is the verb we use to indicate the status and nature of our passions or desires. "To do," on the other hand, is the verb to indicate what we *do* with our passions and feelings.

Broken generations do not come from feelings per se but from wrong actions. This is true for the new generation as well as the older generation. They both are part of the problem. Brokenness not only runs in families but also in generations. Broken families and broken generations are closely connected. They tend to keep each other broken as long as they don't change their actions. The cure for broken generations is restoring their identity by the right actions.

Although generations are interconnected and may pass on their brokenness, there is something peculiar about the latest generation: they are dying at a rate not seen since the Vietnam War. That in itself is shocking, but the most shocking part is they are not dying in combat—they're dying of the effects of drug overdoses, alcoholism, mental illness, depression, and suicide, at a rate 200 percent higher than the 1980s in much of the United States. And it's not just substance addictions that are on the rise: behavioral addictions have also spiked. Pornography addiction in particular has reached what some view as crisis levels.

But a seemingly less serious behavioral addiction for most of us is the use of smartphones and the like. Checking a smartphone is something the average person now does 221 times a day, or every 4.3 minutes, according to a recent study—but the numbers are still on the rise. This habit has even affected the youngest ones among us. They start using them at just over ten years old, and they spend nearly nine hours a day in front of a screen. Nearly three-fourths of teenagers own a smartphone now. A former vice-president at Facebook told an audience recently, "We have created tools that are ripping apart the social fabric." Instead of connecting us, we feel more disconnected than ever. What is considered part of social media is actually making us more asocial. It is hard to believe this makes our identity stronger. But it is also hard to tell whether these tools cause a lack of identity, or reversed, that a lack of identity makes people crave for using these tools.

Instead of tracing addictions back to a lack of willpower, or to a brain disease, it seems to be first of all a spiritual disease that starts when a person feels disconnected from his or her self—and thus from people around them, and ultimately from God. In other words, it seems to be another case of an identity crisis. When you were not given a chance by your parents and your surroundings to develop a healthy and coherent identity, you go on a search for one, chasing for whatever you encounter in the world around you, including drugs. Chances are you end up in a mess and a turmoil.

Of course, there is not one cure-it-all approach for addictions, but an important cure for a messed-up identity is finding your real identity. Not surprisingly, the most successful healing programs available help addicts by encouraging self-reflection and self-evaluation. It turns out, besides, that people are more successful in overcoming addiction when they have an active spirituality in their lives. Spirituality can lead us back to our deepest self, which is the "self" that was made in the image of God. I think I have said it enough: we can't just blame those who belong to the youngest generation. The cure must start before we get to them.

2. A Broken World

An X-Ray of a Broken World

Just as no families are alike, no generations are alike. However, what all generations have in common is that they are broken, although each generation is broken in its own way. How come they *all* are broken? The answer is short and concise: Because they all live in a broken world. The truth is that if we had been presented with the same challenges as our forefathers, most of us would probably have made the same errors. It is a natural human tendency to try to fit in with the group, to go with the flow, to conform, and to avoid risking persecution or exclusion. Apparently, there is something wrong with human nature and the world.

What then is wrong with the world? I know of someone who had a hobby of buying "antique" newspapers and adding them to his collection. One time, he was able to lay his hands on a newspaper some forty years old. He took it to the coffee bar where he usually enjoyed his morning coffee and placed his latest treasure next to his coffee. The person sitting on the stool next to him briefly glanced at the headlines, not knowing it was a very old one, and muttered, "Nothing new again." He was right. The bad news from years ago is not much different from the news we hear today. It does not matter much in which era we live, only the details may vary. The fact is the world is in trouble and has always been in trouble because we all are in trouble. You don't have to be a rocket scientist or brain surgeon to see that there is something wrong with this world—not only now, but also in the past, and most likely in the future as well.

Let us acknowledge first that we do not live in a hedonistic paradise. We should ask ourselves the question: do we really admire those who appear to have a life of ease? What most of us admire, instead, are lives of courage and sacrifice. We have a high regard for people who overcome hardship, deprivation, or weakness so as to achieve some notable success; for people who stand against some great evil, or who relinquish their own pleasures to alleviate the sufferings of others. Apparently, the maximization of creaturely pleasure is not a top priority in most lives and certainly not in the lives of Christians. It is considered part of living in a broken world.

What then is wrong with this world? What causes the world to be broken? Most people would say we are surrounded by evils that cause brokenness in this world. It's *evil* that causes brokenness. That's probably the best explanation of a broken world. But it depends on what we mean by "evil." There are actually two kinds of evil: physical evil and moral evil. *Physical* evil is evil caused by nature—you might think of earthquakes, tsunamis, hurricanes, blizzards, floods, avalanches, diseases, plagues, epidemics, death, and the like. *Moral* evil, on the other hand is evil that humans cause themselves. Let's start with moral evil.

Each one of us is surrounded by moral evils. Not only are we the victims of such evils, but we are also the perpetrators of moral evils. Moral evil is all around us, both on a small and a large scale. We can think of major evils such as the atrocities performed by people like Hitler, Stalin, Mao, bin Laden, or

ISIS. Just think about all those victims of genocide, gas chambers, torture chambers, labor camps, concentration camps, wars, senseless murders—but also of the ones who committed these horrendous crimes.

But then we might forget about all the minor evils very close by. Just to mention the moral evils of sexual harassment, sex trafficking, extramarital affairs, prostitution, rape, pedophilia, and the list goes on and on. Think also of all those neglected by their spouses or their parents or their children—and those who did this to them. So many people had hoped for something good but received so much evil and suffering instead. So many people had hoped to receive a bit more warmth and love, but instead they received none of this. It is moral evil that befalls them, caused by human actions and decisions.

However, there are people who consider the terms "evil" and "sin" as part of an outdated world view. They think we don't *do* anything wrong, but things just *go* wrong—due to genes, hormones, or mere "fate." They make moral evil a case of physical evil. They consider moral evil and sin some kind of disease located somewhere in a gene or temporal lobe or whatever. They even tell us that we have no responsibility whatsoever for our actions by saying that our glands made us act that way. Or they have tried to explain moral evil and sin away as merely a developmental flaw, a psychological weakness, a mistake, or the necessary consequence of an inadequate social structure, and the list goes on and on. But explanations like these miss the point that sin is in essence an abuse of the freedom we have to act either morally right or morally wrong—a violation of the freedom God has given to created persons so that they are, in the words of the Catechism (387), "capable of loving him and loving one another."

By eliminating the term "sin," these people think we can all be taken off the *moral* hook. I would say that's too good to be true. We know deep down this cannot be true. That's the reason why most religious people trace moral evil back to sin. The explanation most Christians would give is that moral evil is caused by sin—ultimately the sin of Adam and Eve in Paradise, which caused the Fall. We will get back to the origin of moral evil later in this chapter.

But what about *physical* evil? Could physical evil also be the cause of brokenness in this world? In other words, how "evil" are physical evils? It seems so obvious that physical evils—such as earthquakes, tsunamis, hurricanes, floods, plagues, diseases, or death—do cause brokenness in this world. So they must be evil! But how obvious is this really?

To call physical or natural events "evil" is actually quite a stretch. Why? Physical events are part of nature and are caused by what we call the "laws of nature." Somehow, nature is bound to "obey" its God-given laws of nature. One simple example of this is that God made a Universe in which small objects would be attracted to larger ones, which we call the force of gravity. Thus we are able to know what the outcome is of certain contingent events like stones falling—we can predict what will happen "if...." This way, we live in a world that makes prediction and anticipation possible because nature follows some God-given, unchangeable laws of nature. This allows meteorologists, astronomers, and biologists to warn us ahead of time, based on sound predictions, of upcoming events. It even helps us make some simple personal predictions and decisions. If I decide to ignore the law of gravity and jump off a cliff, my defiance will not cause gravity to cease working. It causes a physical disaster I asked for myself.

In other words, gravity is something good, not evil—it keeps us put on the earth, for example. But, on the other hand, gravity seems to turn into something bad when a rock falls on my head. But we can't blame gravity for this. Mathematics is also something good—it allows us to calculate and predict. But it turns into something bad when we miscalculate and don't know math well enough. But again, we can't blame math for our miscalculations. And the weather is something good—it gives us the sun, the water, and the air that we depend on. But it also causes floods, mud slides, hurricanes, wild fires, and other disasters. Again, we can't accuse the weather for it. Perhaps we should say the same about God. He gave us gravity, mathematics, and the weather, but we can't blame God for it when we ourselves misuse those gifts.

Yet, just like we blame humans for moral evil, so we tend to blame God for physical evils, because they are usually beyond our control. Why is it then that we cannot blame God for physical evils? We cannot expect God to temporarily suspend his own laws—gravity, math, meteorology—when we wish so. Does this mean God has nothing to do with those disasters? Yes and no. Let me use a simple example: When I cut wood with an ax, I cut the wood, but so does the ax. When cutting wood, I am somehow a "primary cause," and the ax is acting like a "secondary cause." I, as a primary cause, use the ax as a secondary cause—and together we make things happen.

Something similar can be said about God's actions in the world: God can and usually does work in and through natural causes. God is the "primary cause," but the laws of nature and their effects are "secondary causes." Natural causality in the universe and God's divine causality are not mutually exclusive. The first depends upon the second, but they both operate in their own ways—but more importantly, on two completely different levels.

Seen in this light, a force such as gravity is a secondary cause. By allowing an "inferior" cause like this to operate, God made a Universe in which he does not have to be the direct cause of every stone falling to the ground. We do not have to wonder about God's will every time a stone falls to the ground, even if it strikes us on the head. God has given us a secondary cause—the force of gravity—which is the direct cause of each stone's earthly plummet. Something similar can be said about diseases. As floods and drought are a necessary consequence of the fabric of the physical world, predators and parasites, dysfunctions and diseases are a consequence of the biological world and its laws of nature.

Obviously, the forces of nature can cause results that are lovely as well as cruel, and beautiful as well as ugly. Volcanos can create beautiful islands and mountains, but also devastating destruction. The power of growth makes flowers and babies develop into something beautiful, but it also makes tumors get bigger. And the weather may be the cause of a gentle breeze as well as a destructive tornado. It is our task—also given by our Creator—to get more and more control over these forces and make them "work for the good." In the meantime, we should realize that there is a big difference between what God wills and what He allows. God doesn't will earthquakes, but He allows them when they are a consequence of the laws of nature—in the same way as God doesn't will wars but allows them when humans use their freedom to start them.

If all of this is true, then the brokenness of this world is not really caused by the laws of nature—they are basically "neutral." If it is true that natural disasters do not cause a broken world by themselves, then why do we detest earthquakes, tsunamis, hurricanes, floods, diseases, death, and the like so much? What is it that makes natural events sometimes lovely or sometimes cruel, and sometimes beautiful or sometimes ugly? So when we call certain natural events "physical evils," what then could it be that makes them "evil"? The Christian answer would be that all evil, moral or physical, is connected with sin. Most Christians know that we live in a broken world because of *sin*.

What does physical evil have to do with sin? How could sin ever be the origin and cause of natural disasters. We usually associate sin with what *we* do ourselves, not with what the laws of nature do. Sin is usually seen as something humans commit—nature doesn't sin, humans do. Sin and evil do not seem to be something that comes with natural events. And yet they are strongly connected. How can they be connected? The connection can be found in the Original Sin, committed by Adam and Eve in Paradise. Since then, natural events can become physical evil. How is that possible?

Thomas Aquinas makes a very astute remark in this context: "Some say that the animals, which are wild now and kill other animals, were not that way [in paradise ...]. But this is entirely unreasonable. The nature of animals was not changed by the sin of man." Aquinas is right; after the Fall the world did not change, but *we* did. The laws of nature did not change, but *we* did. Without sin, physical evils would not rankle or embitter us. Physical events only become evil when we as human beings assess them as evil and dub them as evil. Only humans take diseases and catastrophes as something that "should" not be—as something "evil."

This explains why there's no physical evil in the animal world, for instance. A prey does not consider the predator "evil"—perhaps painful, literally, but not evil. When giving birth, animals may experience physical pain but not suffering in the sense of something "bad." Humans, on the other hand, do. Only humans can get depressed. Animals may "dislike" these things, but they do not question them in terms of "Why *me*?" They do not have a "me," and since animals do not know about good and bad, they cannot ask why bad things happen to good animals. There is no "evil" in the animal world, and neither is there in the natural world.

Yet, there is *evil* that makes the world broken and troubled. Evil is nothing new, it has always been with us since the beginning of humanity. It is the kind of evil that only humans can commit, for there is no moral evil in the animal world, as we said earlier. Animals do not know about good and evil; they cannot ask why bad things happen to good animals. When animals do seem to do awful things, it is only because we as human beings consider their actions "evil" according to our moral standards. Yet, we will never arrange court sessions for grizzly bears that maul hikers because we know bears are not morally responsible for their actions. Besides, if animals had moral rights, their fellow animals, too, would need to respect those "rights."

The same holds for physical evils. The "thorns and thistles" in nature are a natural part of this world—they are not evil as such. That was even so in Paradise. But since the Fall of Adam and Eve, they have been felt, not only as painful, but also as distressing, as something "evil." So the "thorns and thistles" may have always been there, but since the Fall in Paradise, they were felt as something "evil." The Fall changed some natural events into distressing events and personal disasters. I will repeat—Thomas Aquinas was right: after the Fall the *world* did not change, but *we* did. Because we changed—due to sin—physical events could become distressing evils that can cause a broken world.

For Christians, there is even a much deeper dimension to all of this. Because they know of God and they believe God is a God of love, Christians see everything, including personal disasters, in terms of a personal relationship with God. So they tend to ask the question "Is something wrong between God and me?" or "Why do bad things happen to good people?" Since animals do not know about good and bad, they cannot ask why bad things happen to good animals, but humans certainly can. Is there something wrong between God and me then when afflictions strike me?

To answer this question properly, let us first rephrase the question: If I ask myself why evil strikes *me*, I could ask myself as well why evil would *not* strike me. Realizing suffering is everywhere may help us to de-center from our own suffering. Or consider the example of an infection. Each time we do get an infection, we tend to be upset, but we should rather be surprised that more often we do *not* get an infection. The real wonder comes from our beautifully designed immunity system—another wonderful piece of creation. Being God's co-workers, we may be able to find some medical cures to fight the infection, but infections as such are part of this world. They happen to man and animal alike.

Does all of this mean we should welcome good events but reject bad events? Not really. We would not know of a good outcome if there wasn't such a thing as a bad outcome. Sorrow is the price we pay for joy. Yet it seems to be easier for us to acknowledge sorrowful events over joyful events. Why don't we try to reverse this habit? As a matter of fact, it is because of joyful events that we are able to speak of sorrowful events. Because there is good in this world, we know there is also physical evil in this world—something that *lacks* good. Pain is the absence of joy, death is the absence of life, sickness is the absence of health, tragedy is the absence of fortune. We do not seem to fully appreciate the real gifts of creation—joy, life, health, and fortune—until they are taken away from us. Would we rather not want these gifts out of fear that we might lose them? No, I would say it is better to enjoy them than to have never known them.

After all of this, I think we have the right to say: No, it's not physical evil that causes a broken world. It's not earthquakes, tsunamis, hurricanes, floods, diseases, cancer, death, and the like that cause a broken world. Sin did! Sin made us see them as evil that causes a broken world. A broken world is caused by *us*. It is caused by our own actions—regardless of whether it was in Paradise or still goes on from generation to generation. This shifts the focus from physical evil to its moral dimension, from physical events to moral actions. The surprising outcome of this discussion is that, ultimately, it's moral evil that explains physical evil.

We know of "evil" because we have an idea of "good" and of what things should be like if everything were "good"—the way God intended them to be before the Fall. Evil—and hence suffering—has everything to do with sin. When a paralytic was brought to him, Jesus said, "your sins are forgiven" (Mk 2:5). The paralytic wanted to be healed from his suffering, not to be delivered from his sins, but Jesus saw the man's real need. Forgiveness of sins is the foundation of all true healing. Later on, we will see that only Jesus can heal us from our sins, for he went to Golgotha for each one of us (see Chapter 6).

A Cure for a Broken World?

We live in what is often called a "broken world" or, in the Christian tradition, "a vale of tears." What we try to do about it is to fashion for ourselves another world that is *minus* this brokenness. However, what usually happens as a result of such efforts is that we make things even worse. We wonder why this is so? Why can't we figure ourselves out? We can figure out many things, even about ourselves. Yet, when we do what we can, we will realize that we need help. Who or what could possibly help us? We usually end up with help from people who think that something is wrong with the world but not with themselves. They will spend their days blaming God, culture, possessions, discrimination, or their parents for what is wrong—but never themselves.

Is there a cure for a broken world? It may not be a cure-all therapy, but there is indeed a therapy for a broken world—it's called *morality*. Morality tells us which actions others owe us and which actions we owe others as part of the "common good." Morality is about what "ought" to be done—by us, as a "duty," and towards us, as a "right"—otherwise, a moral mistake would be made. Only morality can steer us right and prevent us from adding more brokenness to a broken world. Unfortunately, there are many misconceptions about what morality stands for.

Misconception #1: morality comes from past experiences. Why is that hard to believe? Well, killing is morally wrong, but certainly not because we discovered so after we had killed some people or had seen some killings. If that were the case, then we would have to do or witness something morally wrong before we can know what is morally right. On the contrary, a moral command comes before what it commands, not after. Moral laws and rules may be corroborated by past experiences, but they are not created by such experiences, and the actual goal is to prevent them.

There is mounting evidence that babies as young as six months old already make moral judgments and can tell right from wrong. Their sense of fairness begins very young. Babies know, for instance, the difference between "good guys" and "bad guys"—despite little or no previous exposure to such situations. Based on this natural feeling of right-and-wrong, they can later be taught something like the more specific "underwear rule" about "bad guys": they should not be touched by others on parts of the body usually covered by their underwear; and they should not touch others in those areas. It is rather telling that children who were sexually abused at a very young age know "intuitively" they had experienced something morally wrong.

Misconception #2: morality comes from the animal world. That is something also hard to defend. Animals do not have morality and cannot act morally or immorally. They do have social behavior, but certainly not moral behavior regulated by a moral code. They just follow whatever "pops up" in their brains—and no one has the right to morally blame them. The relationship between predator and prey, for instance, has nothing to do with morality; if predators really had a conscience guided by a moral code like "Thou shalt not kill," their lives as predators would be pretty harsh.

As I said before, animals never do awful things out of meanness or cruelty, for the simple reason that they have no morality—and thus no cruelty or meanness. When animals do seem to do awful things, it is only because we as human beings consider their actions "awful" according to our standards of morality. Animals do not have moral duties nor do they have moral rights. In other words, animals cannot sin.

Misconception #3: morality comes from our genes. Why would it be hard to claim that our genes tell us what is morally right or wrong? First of all, those who believe that morality is rooted in their genes must face the possibility that this very belief then is also rooted in their genes—which makes it some kind of "boomerang" belief that undermines itself. Second, in the world of genes, there is only material stuff (DNA), but no immaterial truths and untruths—and hence, no intangible moral rights and moral wrongs either. DNA is physical "stuff" that can be long or short, light or heavy, but morals cannot be any of these—they have no mass, size, or color. So it is hard to see how material genes could ever create immaterial moral rules.

Then there is a third reason why morality cannot be in the genes. If morality were in the genes, why would we need articulated moral rules to reinforce what "by nature" we would or would not desire to do anyway? As a matter of fact, if morality were encoded in the genes, a moral code would be completely redundant. Instead the opposite could be argued much better: morality has the power to overrule what our genes dictate—passions, emotions, feelings, and drives. No wonder then that far too many people are willing to break a moral rule when they can get away with it. It is hard to believe they are going against their genes.

Misconception #4: morality is something acquired—through upbringing, training, disciplining, or education. No doubt, discipline is part of morality. People who are at the mercy of their lusts, drives, feelings, and passions may not do the good they ought to do because they are not disciplined enough to resist their lusts. But that doesn't mean morality is nothing more than being educated, taught, and disciplined.

You may compare this with laws of nature, such as the law of gravity. These laws may have to be taught to us in a physics class or biology class, but that doesn't mean laws of nature are only a matter of training and teaching. True, it is partly through schooling that we know about them, but the laws themselves are not a product of schooling. In a similar way, parents may help us understand moral laws better and may help us be better prepared and disciplined to do what is morally right, but that doesn't make what is right and wrong a matter of upbringing.

Misconception #5: morality is a matter of intuition. This is a very common misconception, yet very deceiving. At first sight, it may sound appealing that we know "intuitively" what is right or wrong, but the word "intuition" carries a strong subjective overtone—some may have it, some may not, and some are not "intuitive" at all. That opens it up to the attack that morality is not something real but only exists in a person's mind—famously expressed as "many heads, many minds."

No wonder, then, that intuition is not a very reliable tool to find out what is morally right or wrong. It comes close to "gut feelings." However, "good" is not a matter of what *feels* good. Feelings can never be the standard for judging morality, for we would have to decide next who has the best "gut feelings" or the best "hunch feelings." If so, all defendants in court would be entitled to claim that they just followed their "gut feelings." It is actually the other way around: morality is the standard for judging feelings. Feelings of anger, for instance, need to be curbed by morality before they lead to immoral acts of revenge. Everyone can claim that intuition told him or her what ought to be done, but that does not make such action morally right or wrong.

Misconception #6: morality is a matter of a private conscience. Just as intuition, conscience may seem a good tool in itself to guide our moral behavior. Not surprisingly, it has often been heralded as the ultimate source of moral good and evil. Ironically, even relativists—who deny that morality has any absolute authority—still hold on to at least one moral absolute that says, "Never disobey your own conscience." So they should then ask themselves the question as to where the absolute authority of a human conscience comes from.

How can a person's personal conscience possibly be an infallible guideline for morality? There is no way we can validly justify that our act was morally right by claiming our conscience told us so—even Nazis could make that claim to justify their atrocities. To call one's conscience infallible is at odds with the facts: pro-lifers follow their conscience, as do abortion doctors. Are they both morally right? Only so, if morality were merely a matter of a strictly private conscience—that is, a matter of personal opinions and preferences.

These are six very common misconceptions about morality, and there are probably many more. Now the question arises: where then do moral laws and moral values really come from? There is again some similarity between the laws of nature and the laws of morality. Common sense tells us there is some kind of *physical* order in nature: stones that fall today will also fall tomorrow. Something similar holds for the laws of morality. Common sense tells us there is some kind of *moral* order in life: if murder is wrong today, then it will also be wrong tomorrow. Just as our biological nature makes it necessary for us to eat certain foods and to breathe oxygen for our bodies to be healthy, so our moral nature makes certain moral rules and values necessary for our souls to be healthy.

On the other hand, there is also a striking difference between the two. We may be able to ignore laws of nature but we cannot go against them. However, when it comes to moral laws, we do have the capacity to violate them—for instance, we can violate the moral law that all human life is sacred. When we do so, though, that does not make murder morally right, but it does allow us to neglect or violate a moral law by acting as if no such law exists. Such is possible for the simple reason that there is human *freedom*, which allows us to either follow a moral law or not.

This still leaves the question as to how we know what is morally good or morally wrong. The answer is basically simple: we just know! Much in the same way that we, without musical training, can judge certain tones to be off pitch, so, too, do we have moral knowledge that some actions are good and some bad without having any explicit training about such kinds of actions. Somehow, we just "know" what is morally right or wrong. Just as we know what we do not want others to do to us, so we also know what we should not do to others—which is usually called the Golden Rule, "Do to others what you want to be done to yourself" (Tobit 4:15; Matthew 7:12; Luke 6:31). We use that rule constantly, especially to judge the actions of others (but not always to judge our own actions!).

The Golden Rule is a principle of morality found in many cultures and religions, suggesting it may be a common-sense issue related to a fundamental human nature we all share. True, there are some important disagreements between different cultures about what exactly is "good", but beneath all disagreements about lesser moral laws and values, there always lies an agreement about more basic ones. Peter Kreeft compares this with different languages: beneath the different words of different languages you find common concepts—and this is what makes translation from one language to another possible.

In an analogous way, we find common moral laws beneath different social laws. As a matter of fact, there is not a great deal of difference between Christian morality, Jewish morality, Hindu morality, Muslim morality, or Buddhist morality—although there's a much diversity in these religions. Put differently, every culture in history has had some version of the Ten Commandments. This idea was also expressed by the Apostle Paul when he referred to pagans as people "who never heard of the Law but are led by reason to do what the Law commands" (Rom. 2:14).

The first Christian philosopher, St. Justin Martyr, said something similar already around the year 150 while living in the turbulent, mostly pagan Roman Empire. He made some excellent observations:

> *Every race knows that such things as adultery, and fornication, and homicide are sinful. For example, though they all fornicate, they do not escape from the knowledge that they are acting unrighteously—with the exception of those possessed by an unclean spirit, those debased by wicked customs and sinful institutions, and those who have quenched their natural ideas. For we observe that such persons refuse to endure the same things they inflict on others. They also reproach each other for the evil acts that they commit.*

Back to our original question: Why is our world broken? The main reason is that its inhabitants do *not* follow the rules and laws of morality, but instead follow their own passions and lusts. They did so already in Paradise. They decided not to follow God's Commands, but their own commands. Since then, all that happens to us is seen in terms of good or evil. Apparently it is very hard to follow moral rules because our passions and lusts are so powerful and demand so much immediate attention that moral considerations become easily side-tracked if we are not careful.

So this raises the question of how we can characterize the laws of morality. First of all, they are considered *self-evident*—in the same sense as the *United States Declaration of Independence* could state, "We hold these truths to be self-evident." When people claim they have certain unalienable rights, there is no evidence to support such a claim. When someone asks us why killing another human being is morally wrong, there is nothing we can point to as evidence—it is self-evident, just like it's evident that the whole is greater than any of its parts. Murder is wrong—period! There is no further explanation. Anyone who doesn't see this is "morally blind."

Second, moral laws are also *unconditional.* Most rules with which we are familiar are conditional upon a certain goal: if you want Y, you must do X; if you do not want to attain that goal, the rule is useless. Not so with moral rules and laws. They are unconditional: just do X, for you *ought* to do X—no matter what, whether you like it or not, whether you feel it or not, whether others enforce it or not. Therefore, when it comes to morality, we cannot just pick whatever we want. We cannot just vote to decide whether we condone certain actions—such as slavery and abortion—or rather not. There is no "pro-choice" in morality. Morality obliges us to go, unconditionally, for what is good and right. No more ifs; no more questions asked. Of course, we do have a choice rooted in human freedom to not do what is right.

Third, moral laws are also *objective*: they are a "given" independent of us and of any human authority. In other words, they are not something we invented but something we discovered or could have discovered or may discover someday. "Objective" means that something is real and true, regardless of whether or not we know it to be true. Something similar holds for laws of nature such as the law of gravity. This law has always been true, even before Isaac Newton discovered the law—it was a discovery, not an invention. The same can be said about moral laws; we don't invent them but must discover them; they are not merely a subjective experience but an objective reality. Morality is not a matter of likes and dislikes, but of what is objectively right or wrong. In other words, if we were to create or invent our own moral laws and moral values, then they would not qualify as moral laws or values, and they would not be anchored in reality.

Fourth, moral laws are also *universal*: they are the same for everyone everywhere. They are universally applicable to all of humanity, regardless of race, ethnicity, nationality, culture, religion, or political affiliation. Morality is not connected with interest groups or with majority votes, but it is universal in nature and applies to anyone anywhere. Interestingly enough, without the universality of the laws of morality, there would not have been any justification for the Nuremberg trials that took place after World War II—or for any other international court, for that matter. Those denying the universality of moral laws are basically relativists who privatize and politicize moral laws as if they were merely local civil laws. These moral relativists consider moral laws man-made, private, subjective, a matter of mere feeling—at best a matter of consensus or a majority vote or political decisions.

Fifth, moral laws are also *timeless*, and therefore unchangeable. Not only do they hold for anyone anywhere, but also at any time, past, present, and future. You might ask, though, didn't the moral laws against slavery change over time? Yes, they did, but we should not confuse moral laws and moral *values* with moral *evaluations*. Moral evaluations are only personal feelings or discernments regarding objective moral values and laws at a certain point in time. But when making moral evaluations, we do not create moral values in accordance with these evaluations. Only some people in the past—heroes such as St. Cyprian, St. Gregory of Nyssa, St. John Chrysostom, St. Patrick, St. Anselm, St. Vincent de Paul, to name just a few—were able to discern the objective, intrinsic, and universal value of personal dignity and human rights (as opposed to slavery), whereas many of their contemporaries were blind for this value. Think of the following comparison: we assume there are timeless laws of nature, although we may not yet have fully captured them in our current understanding and in our contemporary evaluations. The law of gravity, for instance, has always been there, even before Newton discovered it. The same holds for moral rules: we may be temporarily "blind" for certain moral rules until someone opens our eyes for what has always been there.

Sixth, in addition to being self-evident and unconditional and objective and universal and timeless, moral laws are also *absolute*—which means they are without exceptions. Killing a human being is always morally wrong; stealing is always morally wrong; lying is always morally wrong—no matter who you are and where you are, regardless of your status in society, and regardless of any other particular circumstances. Moral rules and values are absolutes—unchanging rocks beneath the changing waves of feelings, practices, and evaluations. This also means they are absolute in the sense that they cannot be validated by anything "relative." Nevertheless, it is very tempting to use relative criteria for absolute moral rules and values. This is done, for instance, in the abortion debate with arguments like these: the more brain activity there is, the more value an unborn child has; the more developed the baby is, the more protection it deserves. However, the biological criteria adduced here are relative, not absolute criteria, and thus become moving targets. So they do not make for moral but at best quasi-moral arguments.

So we must come to the conclusion that moral laws—often collectively called the *natural law*—are universal (applicable to everyone everywhere), absolute (without exceptions), timeless (even if we do not know the underlying law yet), and objective (a given, independent of us and of any human authority). Just as "truths are true," even when we do not know yet they are true, so "rights are right," even though we may not realize yet they are morally right. Think of the following. In order to calculate the surface of triangles, the ancient Egyptians used a formula that is obviously wrong compared with our kind of geometry; yet, for centuries, this formula was useful. This does not prove, of course, that there are two correct formulas for calculating the surface of triangles on earth. It proves only that humans in those days did not know yet the right formula. The very same conclusion holds also for the domain of morality.

How can moral laws be all of the above? How can they be the therapy to heal a broken world? The answer is that they receive their power from the Maker of Heaven and Earth. The Creator created a world with a physical order as well as a moral order. Going against the moral order is as destructive to the world as going against its physical order. If moral laws did not come from God, then they would be literally baseless—they would have no foot to stand on. They would just be arbitrary rules made up by people, perhaps implemented by a government, but nevertheless a matter of mere feelings and opinions. If that were true, relativists would be right: there would be nothing absolute, universal, timeless, and objective about them. We would have no good reason to accept, let alone implement, them. Those kind of moral laws would not have the power to better a broken world.

Even a few astute atheists have been aware of this fact. The late French philosopher and nearly life-long atheist Jean-Paul Sartre, for instance, realized that there can be no absolute and objective standards of right and wrong if there is no eternal Heaven that would make moral laws and rules objective and universal. By denying the existence of God, Sartre realized very clearly that he also had to give up on morality. If there is no God, there cannot be evil either—there could not even be a broken world. Sartre saw very clearly that, without God, there is no morality.

The German philosopher Friedrich Nietzsche was another atheist to realize how devastating the decline of religion is to the morality of society. He described how societies without God shelter themselves in caves and venerate shadows of the God they once believed in; they are still holding on to something they cannot provide themselves, mere shadows of the past. These have now become mere "idols" constructed to preserve the essence of morality without the substance. This does not mean, of course, that people must believe in God in order to live a moral life. As Nietzsche put it, they can still venerate "idols from the past."

Their argument, succinctly, is that for an objective moral system to exist, God must exist. A culture that cannot name God also cannot name evil for what it is. The writer Fyodor Dostoyevsky had it right when he said, "Without God, all things are permissible." For a moral system to be truly objective, moral law must stem from a source transcending humanity. Otherwise, all we have left is subjective human moral opinion, no matter how it is dressed up. Thus we end up with merely private opinions in all matters moral and religious. The implications of this are particularly shocking, especially since the vast majority of nonbelievers live and act as if they believe in an objective moral system while their own belief system makes this logically impossible, or at least inconsistent.

There is actually no alternative to base morality on but God. Some think utilitarianism is a viable alternative. It considers something morally right depending on its effects—that is, if it leads to "the greater happiness of a greater number of people." However, this alternative is merely a philosophical theory invented by man. For even if every person on earth accepted utilitarianism, no one would be obligated to follow it in the same way that we are obligated to follow the moral law of the Creator of Heaven and Earth. For if God does not exist, then who is to say whether it is right or wrong to follow these human inventions, including utilitarianism?

Because of all of this, we must recognize that, ultimately, morality can only come from "Above." Moral laws and values reside in Heaven. That's where their universality and objectivity reside. We ought to do what we ought to do—for Heaven's sake! This is actually the only way to explain why morality can be such a demanding issue—indeed demanding an absolute authority. This would be impossible if morality were only a matter of genes, or tradition, or majority votes, or political correctness. Do my genes, or any other natural factors, have the right to demand absolute obedience from me? Of course not! Does society or the government have the right to demand my absolute obedience? Certainly not! Does any person have the right to demand my absolute obedience?

None of the above! The only authority that can obligate me is someone infinitely superior to me; no one else has the right to demand my absolute obedience.

The *United States Declaration of Independence* is in tune with this when it declared that we are endowed by our Creator with certain unalienable Rights—not man-made but God-given rights, that is. When in 1948 the United Nations (UN) affirmed in its *Universal Declaration of Human Rights* that, "all human beings are born free and equal in dignity and rights," it must have assumed the same without explicitly mentioning it (the drafters famously left the term "right" vague in order to achieve passage). Without this assumption, all those rights would be sitting on quicksand, subject to the mercy of law makers and majority votes. The Catholic philosopher Jacques Maritain expressed a profound truth when he said paradoxically, "We agree on these rights, on condition that no one asks us why." Well, the only reason why we do have human rights is because God has endowed us with rights.

In his book *Mere Christianity,* C.S. Lewis clearly and beautifully explained that calling the world cruel (physical evil) and unjust (moral evil) must already assume that we have a moral and spiritual standard deriving from Heaven—and that is the place where God resides. Asserting "evil exists" necessarily implies a moral standard against which to define good and evil; and such a standard implies the existence of God. Without God, we couldn't even speak of evil. Thanks to God, we know what the world "should" be like. We know of "evil" because we have an idea of "good" and of what things should be like, if everything indeed were "good." Without that idea, we could not even speak of a "broken world." It may sound strange at first sight, but without God there could not be a broken world—actually not even a world. But again, the brokenness of this world is not God's doing but ours!

So how can we do our part to heal, or at least diminish and limit, the brokenness of this world? I think the best way—and perhaps the only way—is by restoring our God-given morality and its Ten Commandments. This is certainly not the morality as understood by relativists who claim we have no way of *knowing* that something is morally wrong or not. Ironically, it's precisely the morally relativistic perspective modern culture has instilled in us with the goal of making us "tolerant" that has resulted in so much intolerance.

Relativists never learned to discuss moral judgments and judge them with a clear mind, because they consider them merely a matter of opinions. Therefore, instead of reasoned argument and discussion, you get screaming mobs and broken glass. Even when relativists say we must be "inclusive," they reject all those they consider not inclusive—which is not very inclusive, of course. That's when tolerance usually turns into intolerance. All opinions are considered equal—but some are more equal than others, in this view. How is it possible for people whose main goal in life is to be "open" and "tolerant" regarding other people's views to be the same people screaming bloody murder at those whose views differ from theirs?

We should ask moral relativists: is slavery okay, is abortion okay, is rape okay, is violence okay? The answer cannot be just a matter of how we *feel*. Feelings merely indicate the status and nature of our passions or desires. The old Latin adage had it right: "About taste there is no dispute." Feelings are something you either have or you don't—they cannot be true or false, let alone morally right or wrong. Instead, in morality, everyone has something they *know* is morally wrong. The irony is that relativists are very selective; they use relativism to be very judgmental about things they don't like, such as racism and slavery, but abortion they consider okay. Feelings don't make things right or wrong. Instead, we should know what is right and wrong.

If this is true—and relativists are wrong—then the therapy for a broken world is virtue, not vice. Virtue is what we need back again, not vice. Virtue stands for the good deeds and thoughts of humans whereas vice indicates the bad or evil side of human beings. St. Bernard of Clairvaux was once asked what the three most important virtues are. He famously replied, "Humility, humility, and humility."

Virtues and vices are not characteristics that are inborn. When we grow older, we can cultivate virtues and, unfortunately, also vices. Virtues come with high moral standards. Love, compassion, kindness, charity, courage, loyalty, justice, etc. are some examples of virtues. Virtues bring happiness and goodness to a broken world, because they are in line with the moral order of this world. In contrast, if a person cultivates vices, those bring dishonor or rejection and thus add to a broken world: cruelty, murder, unkindness, greed, vindictiveness, malice, and so on.

A broken world would benefit immensely from people who cultivate virtue instead of vice. The Catechism (1803) has this to say about virtues: "A virtue is an habitual and firm disposition to do the good." Virtues are the cures a broken world badly needs. Without morality, we keep piling up vices and evils.

3. A Broken Family

An X-Ray of a Broken Family

One of the reasons—and not an insignificant one—for the fact that we live in a broken world is that there are so many broken families. There have always been broken families—caused by war, for instance. But a broken family is more than a family that fell apart through forces from "outside," beyond our control. There are also disintegrating forces coming from "within." Lately, there has emerged a new cause of broken families, this time coming from both the "outside" and the "inside": a different view on human sexuality.

Sexuality forms an important part of human life, especially family life. Two of the Ten Commandments refer explicitly to sexual matters: #6 "You shall not commit adultery," and #9 "You shall not covet your neighbor's wife." I know of a priest who would routinely speak about sins against the 6th and 9th Commandment, so he was commonly known as "six-by-nine." That may have been a jibe, but there is something to it: the importance of sexuality is undeniable in human life. It is the area in which many nuclear families are broken, or never came to exist: infidelity, divorce, unwed pregnancies, single parenthood, abortion. A different view on sexuality has become one of the main threats to the nuclear family, and thus to the entire generation, and ultimately to the entire world.

So what is this new view that has revolutionized human sexuality? It has been pointed out repeatedly that this new trend is connected with the "sexual revolution" which has aimed to liberate humanity from any sexual restraints. Its origin can probably be traced back to Sigmund Freud, who made us believe that we suffer psychologically when we suppress our sexual desires. He was not the first one, of course, to discover the lust of the flesh—Adam and Eve were, long before him—but Freud glorified it, teaching us that we must be liberated from old taboos regarding sex with a "simple" motto: always follow your sexual desires!

Very recently, however, we saw a dramatic twist in the debate about marriage and sexuality. The so-called "sexual revolution," unleashed in the 1960s, aimed to "liberate" human sexuality from the straightjacket of "traditional" morality, specifically the perceived "restrictive" morality of marriage in Christianity. The groundwork had been laid in the 1940s by Alfred Kinsey, who did what he called "scientific research" on human sexuality, published in his so-called "Kinsey Reports." But lo and behold, the supposedly "disinterested, impartial observers" of his team were encouraged by Kinsey to sexually experiment with each other, himself, his wife, and invited guests. Not surprisingly, some have speculated that Kinsey was just driven by his own sexual lusts; some have actually called him a pervert.

Yet many others praised Kinsey's "insights." He also inspired, among many others, the founder of *Playboy* magazine, Hugh Hefner. Hefner's former girlfriend, Holly Madison, said about him that while she lived in the Playboy Mansion, Hefner "would encourage competition—and body image issues—between his multiple live-in girlfriends." She added, "His legacy is full of evidence of the exploitation of women for professional gain." Hefner knew very well how to cloak his predatory designs in the language of sexual progressivism.

Although Kinsey died in 1956 and Hefner in 2017, we are still living with the consequences of their actions. Since then, many have come to see sexuality as completely liberated from the bonds of marriage, monogamy, love, and fidelity. This is even reflected in the way news reports from the BBC, for instance, shifted their terminology from "committing adultery" to "being unfaithful," and soon thereafter to "having an affair." That's what the sexual liberation has done for us.

Up until the sexual revolution, each generation had similar expectations: that one would grow up to have children and a family and that one would have parents and siblings. But such expectations would soon, and rapidly, be erased by the sexual revolution—which made the universal human question of "Who am I?" harder to answer. No longer is it clear who my brother or sister is, and who my father is. This loss of clarity has driven these days the frenzied search for identity we talked about earlier—"Who am I?" As Mary Eberstadt, a former Senior Fellow at Stanford University's Hoover Institution, remarks,

> *An illiterate peasant of the Middle Ages was better equipped to answer that question than many people in advanced societies in this century. He may only have lived until age thirty—but he spent his days among family and in towns, practicing a shared faith, and thus developed a vivid sense of those to whom he was elementally connected, not just in the course of his life but before birth and after death.*

The effects of the sexual revolution are devastating. Here are some numbers, if you haven't been convinced yet. According to a 2005 Kaiser Family Foundation study, the number of sexual scenes on television has almost doubled since 1998. Seventy percent of all shows have some sexual content—averaging five sexual scenes per hour compared to 56% and 3.2 scenes per hour, respectively, in 1998. There are nearly 600,000 registered sex offenders in the United States today. However, as many as 150,000 are "lost" in the system, having failed to comply with registration duties and thus remain undetected due to law enforcement's inability to track their whereabouts. Half of all Christian men and 20% of all Christian women are addicted to pornography. Sixty percent of the women who answered the survey admitted to having significant struggles with lust; 40% admitted to being involved in sexual sin in the past year, and 20% of church-going female participants struggle with looking at pornography on an ongoing basis.

More than ever, we need to counteract the effects of this "sexual revolution." We need to escape from behind enemy lines of the sexual revolution. At the moment "love" is detached from marriage it becomes a menace and turns into "lust." This same love—or actually lust—makes people leave their families and neglect their moral duties. The fact is that love in itself can create practically incurable wounds when it is refused, trampled upon, or not returned. Love is like a beautiful river that turns into a menacing torrent once it exceeds its bounds. Yet, this very love urges people to make one of the most important decisions in life: the decision to marry, to take another's side for good, to share every part of life from now on with one's significant other. In fact, love is the only valid reason to do so. Otherwise, having the other person always around will gradually become more and more of a nuisance.

As a consequence of the sexual revolution, we have become a

generation ruled by Viagra, prostitution, pornography, sexual abuse, and rape. As Peter Kreeft points out, this so-called "revolution" has only led to growing numbers of children who are sexually abused and women who are beaten, abandoned, or raped by men who do not want to hear about self-control and who consider every subject they meet as a mere object for their own use or abuse. We don't have to look far—it's all over the news and the internet. We witness now a deluge in sexual harassment cases—coming from Hollywood, Congress, mass media. And that is probably only the tip of the iceberg. I know things like these are not really new and did happen before—they took place for decades in schools, in the military, and even in the Church—but they were considered sins, whereas they are seen as "rights" nowadays. There is no denying, sexual harassment has become a devastating avalanche.

Not only has the sexual revolution led to numerous and various kinds of sexual harassment, but it has also affected the marriage bond in nuclear families. For centuries, sex had been for two things at the same time—for pleasure and for new life. But now the sexual revolution has made sure that sex would be only for fun by eliminating the possibility of new life. This new ideology started a booming industry of contraceptives that would make this "dream" come true. But it led to many more consequences.

One of them was an alarming rise of divorces. What they called "love"—from now on understood as sexual "fun"—could now be found anywhere with anyone, except for the one you are married to. One of the songs Dean Martin used to sing was "With the Small Exception of Me." The words are heartbreaking:

Everybody knows you are leaving me for good.

Everyone tells me now they knew you would. It's a well-known secret I just couldn't see, And the whole world knew with the small exception of me.

Sad songs like these are also at the heart of much classical country/western music. Take the lyrics of "The Tennessee Waltz":

I was dancing with my darling to the Tennessee Waltz / when an old friend I happened to see. / I introduced her to my loved one, / and while they were dancing, / my friend stole my true love from me.

Divorce is undoubtedly a major cause of broken families. A few decades ago it was often said—inspired by ideas from the sexual revolution—that kids were better off when their unhappy parents divorced. In this view, the happiness of kids is important, but the (sexual) happiness of their parents is still seen to be more important. Kids should be willing, so the reasoning goes, to sacrifice a share of their happiness in order that Mom and Dad can engage in their own pursuit of unlimited happiness. Nowadays, however, the tide seems to be turning; you hear more and more the opposite claim that, with exceptions here and there, kids are worse off when their parents separate. Mary Ellen Stanford asks the pivotal question:

Can today's adults—so very fixed on trying to find fulfilment through sex—accept the truth that they can survive without sex, but that children cannot thrive without the fullness of Christian marriage?

At the moment intercourse doesn't need the context of marriage anymore, and marriage need no longer to be directed toward the rearing of the next generation, marriage gets in trouble, ready for a speedy decline. The sexual revolution has separated what is essential to marriage: the unison of the two parents and the creation of a new generation. The child draws husband and wife together. Once we deliberately leave the child out of a marriage, we separate these two functions of a marriage, so that sex is now only for sexual satisfaction and no longer for bringing new life into the world. While sex-for-pleasure involves two individuals seeking their own satisfaction, sex-for-procreation involves two individuals coming together in the most intimate way to produce another human being. Separate them, and the family is in trouble.

Without any doubt, pleasure—including sexual pleasure—plays an important role in our lives and in marriage. If eating food and having sex did not stimulate feelings of pleasure and reward, we would die out. Our brains are wired to ensure that we will repeat life-sustaining activities by associating those activities with pleasure or reward. The limbic system, which contains the brain's reward circuit, is activated when we perform pleasurable activities. It makes for an intersection where all pleasure-related behaviors meet. This explains why sexuality is such a powerful force. The question is, though, where sexuality has its proper place—inside or outside the marriage.

Desires, feelings, emotions—sometimes called "the passions"—all have an important place in married life. But because sexual passion is the strongest and most attractive of all passions, it is also the most addictive and the most blinding. Therefore, there is no more powerful undermining of our moral knowledge and our moral life than the sexual revolution. But how long will this revolution last? The day is coming when more and more people damaged by the false promises of the sexual revelation will find themselves desperately seeking a moral promise that they can finally trust.

In the meantime, this so-called revolution keeps doing its work. It affects almost every aspect of morality and has contributed greatly to an increase in sex outside marriage, in unwed pregnancies, abortion, single parenthood, cohabitation, divorce, poverty, sex trafficking, the exploitation of women, and declining marriage rates. Not surprisingly, this has affected the way new, young, and vulnerable family members see themselves. Unfortunately, a broken world breeds broken families, and broken families create broken hearts. That's how brokenness propagates.

The underlying problem is that we do have a free choice when it comes to morality: we can give in to our sexual desires, or we can resist and control them. But when it comes to morality, a freedom of choice does not mean we can choose whatever we want. We cannot vote to decide whether we are anti-slavery and anti-abortion, or not. Slavery, which seems to be such a clear case, was legal in the United States a short time ago. What has changed? Law professor Robert George likes to ask his college students how many of them, if they lived in the South before the Civil War, would have opposed slavery. They all raise their hands. "Bless their hearts," says he, and tells them what their opposition would have cost them: ridicule, slander, or much worse. It is so easy to take a relativistic stance, even more so in hindsight. Had the slaveholders won the Civil War, we might today view slavery as an admirable institution, so the reasoning goes.

This kind of relativism has become so popular because it seems so reasonable. Let us apply this approach to more recent times. Had we lived in Nazi Germany, we would all be an Oskar Schindler or a Corrie ten Boom; we would never have been infected by the nationalist and socialist disease. Really? It is hard to believe, since this requires, as Anthony Esolen describes it,

> *[S]elf-surgery without anesthesia: to tear some feature of your errant culture out of your flesh. [...] You have to embrace an authority over against what everybody knows, what everybody says, what everybody does; and this authority must do more than recommend. It must command, even in the face of suffering, doubt, and failure.*

In other words, when it comes to morality—also, or even more so, in the nuclear family—we cannot just choose whatever we want. We are under a higher Authority, in spite of the fact that many claim nowadays that there is no authority higher than "Me, Myself, and I," especially in sexual matters. Each one of us has become his own authority. That is exactly how Eve was tempted in Paradise, "You will be like God, knowing good and evil" (Gen. 3:5). This attitude tells you to enforce your own authority against God and enjoy to the fullest whatever you desire. *You* are in charge, even if it creates a broken family! Can that be true?

A Cure for a Broken Family?

Is there a therapy for the destructive sexualization we are facing nowadays? Yes, there is—it's called *self-control*. Without self-control we do not rise above the level of animals who live by their instincts, emotions, and fears, especially their instinct to seek pleasure and flee pain. What is so nice about being an animal is that they can do whatever pops up in their head without any further restraints. They have no moral code and cannot sin. But humans are different. They have the capacity to sin because they were given the capacity of self-control.

In this context, the Catechism uses the word "temperance," which stands for the virtue of self-control. In its own words (1809):

> *Temperance [self-control] is the moral virtue that moderates the attraction of pleasures and provides balance in the use of created goods. It ensures the will's mastery over instincts and keeps desires within the limits of what is honorable. The temperate [self-controlled] person directs the sensitive appetites toward what is good and maintains a healthy discretion.*

This is where morality comes back in. Morality is not ruled by passions; instead, passions need to be controlled by morality before they destroy ourselves and our society. What are these so-called passions, according to the Catechism (1763, 1767, 1768)?

> *Feelings or passions are emotions or movements of the sensitive appetite that incline us to act or not to act in regard to something felt or imagined to be good or evil.*
>
> *In themselves passions are neither good nor evil. They are morally qualified only to the extent that they effectively engage reason and will. Passions are said to be voluntary, "either because they are commanded by the will or because the will does not place obstacles in their way." It belongs to the perfection of the moral or human good that the passions be governed by reason.*
>
> *Strong feelings are not decisive for the morality or the holiness of persons; they are simply the inexhaustible reservoir of images and affections in which the moral life is expressed. Passions are morally good when they contribute to a good action, evil in the opposite case.*

Unlimited searching for pleasure and for whatever satisfies their passions makes people over-dosed, over-loaded, over-eaten, and over-sexed, opening the gateway for extramarital affairs and for addictions such as pornography and prostitution. Apparently, we need to learn how to keep pleasure within its healthy, natural limits, exerting control over excess by self-discipline—a skill which must be learned as early as possible, since it is not inborn. As long as society keeps telling parents, and parents keep showing their children, that sex is only for pleasure and fun, the character formation of our next generation will be in jeopardy. It is the "perfect" recipe for broken families—a recipe promoted by mass media and social media.

Hopefully, our parents started us on the right path when they taught us delayed gratification—choosing a delayed, larger reward over an immediate, smaller reward. Training our desires is like training our muscles—initially fatigued, we become stronger over time with frequent exercise. Here obviously lies an important task for parents—it's called *parenting*. Parenting is an important cure to heal or, better even, to prevent broken families.

Parenting means that parents are heavily involved in the upbringing and socialization of their children. They can't leave socialization up to the so-called social media. Social media provide an uncontrolled source of upbringing and of acquiring values, which makes it a hindrance to developing an identity. We can't just consume information, we must also select information to nurture our true identity. Therefore, it is an important part of parenting to place limits upon the use of social media—for instance, through using filters or implementing a smartphone curfew or taking social-media breaks. But first of all, we need to learn once again to talk to one another.

The stories and examples parents give to their children help them understand who they are and how they should deal with challenges in everyday life. Thus parents hand on to their children the moral and religious values and customs they had received from their own parents. Failure to do so is one of the main causes of creating a broken generation. Sometimes parents refuse to pass on these values, often because they were told by their surroundings to be suspicious of the values they had received themselves. Once they lose confidence in the values with which they were brought up, they become adrift, and so do their children. Such parents have just come to mistrust tradition, period, and therefore reject child-rearing practices used by previous generations.

When that becomes a general trend, and that seems to be happening right now, schools tend to take over this task with therapeutic councilors and chill-out rooms. They actually "re-educate" their students—not so much with moral and religious values but with so-called life skills of how to deal with emotions such as poor grades, criticism, rejection, and aggression. What gets lost in the process is providing the new generation with the moral and religious resources they need to make their way in the world.

However, parenting requires a "functional" family to begin with. Not too long ago, the term "*dysfunctional* family" came into vogue. As a matter of fact, literally millions of people have grown up in dysfunctional families—that is, in families without functioning fathers and/or mothers. Unfortunately, as the saying goes, you can choose your friends, but you can't choose your family. Characteristics of a dysfunctional family may include alcoholic or drug-addicted parents, physically, emotionally or sexually abusive parents, psychologically disturbed parents, excessively rigid or controlling parents, unconcerned parents, or just plainly absent parents.

It's sad to see how many kids have to grow up with an absent parent, an aloof parent, or an abusing parent. Because they don't know what "normal" is, a dysfunctional family is participating in the pretense that they are a normal family bringing up children within the range of what is considered "normal." Usually, it isn't until their teen years, when kids have spent a considerable amount of time with the families of friends, that they may have a chance to understand that things can be different from what they have experienced in their own families. By that time, they have spent all of their formative years in an abnormal situation, developing abnormal ideas about love, loyalty, interdependence, functioning, and roles. Obviously, that's where parenting has gone off track.

Parenting requires some instruction. Many things we do or own come with an instruction book. Your car has a manual, and before you drive a car you even must get a "learner's permit." Then you must study and pass a couple of tests before you are allowed to legally drive that car. Most tools in our household come with instruction manuals, too. But what about parenting—do you have a book that tells you how to do that? Well, of course you do! As Christians we can look to the Bible for a full set of instructions on how to be parents, and how to be children. The prophet Malachi (3:24) tells us in a nutshell, "He will turn the heart of fathers to their sons, and the heart of sons to their fathers."

Here are a few lines from the Bible for *parents* as to how to treat their children (but there are many more):

> *Take to heart these words which I command you today. Keep repeating them to your children. Recite them when you are at home and when you*

> *are away, when you lie down and when you get up (Deut. 6:6-7).*
>
> *God sets a father in honor over his children; a mother's authority he confirms over her sons (Sir. 3:2).*
>
> *Fathers, do not exasperate your children; instead, bring them up in the training and instruction of the Lord (Eph. 6:4).*
>
> *Fathers, do not embitter your children, or they will become discouraged (Col. 3:21).*

Here are a few lines for *children* as to how to treat their parents (but again, there are many more):

> *My son, take care of your father when he is old; grieve him not as long as he lives. Even if his mind fail, be considerate of him; revile him not all the days of his life; kindness to a father will not be forgotten (Sir. 3:12-14).*
>
> *Those who honor their father will have joy in their own children, and when they pray they are heard. Those who respect their father will live a long life; those who obey the Lord honor their mother (Sir. 3:5-6).*

More and more parents seem to think nowadays that parenting is a matter of giving children a "vote." The concepts of authority and hierarchy have become suspect in modern society. However, when parents give up their parental authority, they set their children adrift, for children need firm guidance to begin with. When their parents don't provide it, they look to peers or the internet. As medical practitioner and psychologist Leonard Sax, MD, puts it, "Legitimate authority establishes a stable moral universe for children." If that's missing, their moral universe becomes shaky.

The psychologist Diana Baumrind has found that the most effective parents, as measured by long-term outcomes, are those who are both strict and loving. But she has also found that many of today's parents don't understand that "strict" and "loving" can and must go together; otherwise, their children end up drifting. Empirical evidence has proven that the sexual revolution has had disastrous effects on children and families. The psychiatrist Rick Fitzgibbons, M.D. testifies to this: "Over the past forty years as a busy psychiatrist, on many days I have felt like an army medic on a battlefield littered with severely wounded adults, teens, and children who have been used as sexual objects by other adults or by their peers."

Dysfunctional, broken families tend to create broken children who have an "inflated sense of self"—which is technically called *narcissism*. People with an inflated sense of self are manipulative and become easily angry, especially when they don't receive the attention they consider their birthright. We see it happen in spoiled brats, but also in their parents from whom they received this inflated sense of self. A leading academic psychologist on narcissism, Dr. Jean Twenge, has examined this serious personality disorder in young people. She has rightly entitled her book *The Narcissism Epidemic*. Many young people have absorbed this model through exposure to the same personality weakness in one or both parents—or were never taught by their parents how to grow in virtues of generosity and self-control so as to overcome it. Parents should teach their children real virtues—not the latest trends in social thought. Virtues determine how you live your life—for instance, by giving to charity or helping your neighbor. Virtues are very different from opinions that you happened to find somewhere else and that you like to broadcast to the world—for instance, by making a social media post voicing support for the cause of the day. Narcissism is a vice, not a virtue.

In order to prepare ourselves for life, we need to learn how to control our appetites, passions, and emotions. Life is not always fun and pleasure. The more one is prepared for that inevitable fact of life, the lower the chances are of falling into a depression, easily followed by an addiction. However, the tools of self-control and self-discipline have to be mastered, and you have a better chance in life if your parents have already helped you and taught you to acquire them. No one likes discipline, but the reality is that we do not live in a hedonistic paradise. As the philosopher Hugh J. McCann puts it, this world is not a place in which comfort and convenience are maximized, in which everyone has an electrode implanted to cause intense euphoria and ecstasy in the limbic system with a simple push of the button.

Training in self-discipline cannot start early enough. Training our desires through self-discipline is like training our muscles—initially fatigued, we become stronger over time with frequent exercise. Children who do not learn the meaning of the word "no" will be at the mercy of impulses and desires they do not know how to control. They turn into spoiled and demanding little tyrants who have not learned that there is a higher authority—at first, the authority of parents, but ultimately the authority of God's moral laws. Not having learned the meaning of constraint could scar them for life.

Unfortunately, self-control has become a "dirty" word in modern society. Many nowadays—mainly as a result of the sexual revolution—glorify freedom from any restraints, so they do not want to hear about self-control. Gabriele Kuby, a

German sociologist and a Catholic convert, has produced a masterly book, *The Global Sexual Revolution: Destruction of Freedom in the Name of Freedom*, in which she documents the deliberate and systematic destruction of the innocence of children, especially in the West, which has been politicized through an intense sexualization process by government-sponsored educational programs. The central thesis of her book is that human freedom is being destroyed in the name of freedom—that is, by a mad quest for absolute freedom, which is leading to a new form of totalitarianism. What this has led to is that even peaceful demonstrations on behalf of family values need heavy police protection nowadays. Ironically enough, the destruction of the nuclear family was a key goal of the Communist movement. No wonder, then, that the first sexual revolution was launched by Vladimir Lenin, with laws legalizing divorce (1918), abortion (1920), and euthanasia (1922).

More than ever do we need to reaffirm that sex belongs to the domain of marriage, monogamy, love, and fidelity; that sex is for new life, not only for fun; that the taming of the sex drive and the proper direction of its energies are necessary conditions for social stability and long-term human happiness. They are the necessary backbone of the nuclear family. Once we separate sex from its life-changing, life-giving potential, we will come to see it as just another want, a desire like any other.

In the nuclear family, a man and a woman make a mutual commitment of radical, self-sacrificial love before God and man. But this pledge is not just a contractual thing; it's not a mutual agreement of good thoughts and good times; it's neither just a merging of households and bank accounts. This pledge is a total mutual commitment of one's self to the other's self so as to have, hold, love, trust, support, and aid each other as well as the fruits of this unity. Pope John Paul II famously exclaimed, "The family is the basic cell of society. It is the cradle of life and love, the place in which the individual is born and grows." It creates a triangle of love. As G. K. Chesterton put it, "This triangle of truisms, of father, mother and child, cannot be destroyed; it can only destroy those civilizations which disregard it." Chesterton also says, "If a triangle breaks out of its three sides, its life comes to a lamentable end." See what happens: disrupt the family and you will disrupt the future.

Unfortunately, recent movies coming from Hollywood have brainwashed us by showing mainly how the nuclear family has been disintegrating. If they do portray a nuclear family, it's a very dysfunctional family. And then it's always a family that does not go to church, which is probably a good point the makers of these movies are unknowingly making—that going to church may keep the family together. As the saying goes, a family that prays together stays together. St. John Chrysostom called the family "the domestic Church." As a matter of fact, the family is the cornerstone of society. The Catechism (2207) calls the family "the original cell of social life":

> *The family is the original cell of social life. It is the natural society in which husband and wife are called to give themselves in love and in the gift of life. Authority, stability, and a life of relationships within the family constitute the foundations for freedom, security, and fraternity within society. The family is the community in which, from childhood, one can learn moral values, begin to honor God, and make good use of freedom. Family life is an initiation into life in society.*

As Peter Kreeft remarks, "[S]ocieties have survived with very bad political systems and very bad economies, but not without strong families." Families are grounded in the rights and duties of a marriage. The parents vow to each other: Only if you marry me and stand by me, can you count on me to bear and help raise your children. In other words, if you do *not* marry me, I owe you nothing.

But there is another consequence. When the sexual revolution made the birth of a child the physical choice of the mother—by providing contraception, and if that did not work, abortion—the sexual revolution also made marriage and child support a social choice of the father. No wonder, the man—actually the father who is not the husband—feels no longer responsible for an unplanned pregnancy. The end result is that many women find themselves less able than ever to get married, stay married, and have a family.

Obviously, marriage and monogamy require a commitment on both sides—no involvement without commitment. The fact that sex can result in a pregnancy has been the most powerful reason for centuries that minimally responsible people have waited until marriage to have sex. When that possibility is annulled, people have sex outside of marriage, babies are born outside of marriage, people prepare poorly for marriage, and marriages break up easily, etc. Men, women, and children alike are all losers in this scenario.

Family is to society what cells are to a body. The truth is that the family is the first place where children learn life's most important lessons. The family is the first place where children find protection and learn the role of being a male or female. None of these "lessons" are inborn; they must be taught and nurtured! Pope Emeritus Benedict XVI stressed the importance of the family because within the family exists, as he put it,

> *[T]he authentic setting in which to hand on the blueprint of human existence. This is something we learn by living it with others and suffering it with others.*

There is indeed strong scientific evidence that children who spend their childhood years with their married biological parents have fewer cognitive, behavioral, and emotional problems than children who did not. Too many children grow up with an absent parent. Do not take this the wrong way: There are perfectly good single parents who raise perfectly fine children. Yet, we should not forget that one of the best predictors of poverty is a broken family life.

It is usually in the family that children learn what is right and wrong—and this process begins at a very simple level. Rushing to the crib every time a child cries may train them to expect instant gratification. Children who do not learn the meaning of the word "no" will be at the mercy of impulses and desires they do not know how to control. They become the tyrants and rulers of the family. They have not learned that there is a higher authority that you just do not question. They have not learned the meaning of constraint. They have not been disciplined. The word "discipline" sounds rigid and may remind some of spanking. But there is a "humane" alternative to spanking kids—grounding them with *timeouts*; soon even the threat of a timeout is already effective, if followed by an explanation of why their behavior was bad.

Just as children learn to imitate language and gestures, they also mimic the moral practices they see at home. The Catechism (2207) calls the family "the community in which, from childhood, one can learn moral values, begin to honor God, and make good use of freedom." The popular saying, garbage in, garbage out, applies even here—and might also apply to what happens in dysfunctional families. Children do need and deserve a functional family. Good role models are essential, thus making every day a "school day" when it comes to moral development. Children who have never learned to be ashamed of certain behaviors are in real trouble, perhaps even for the rest of their lives. In the words of the Catechism (1632):

> *It is imperative to give suitable and timely instruction to young people, above all in the heart of their own families, about the dignity of married love, its role and its exercise, so that, having learned the value of chastity, they will be able at a suitable age to engage in honorable courtship and enter upon a marriage of their own.*

Earlier, we talked about virtues and vices. Virtues and vices are not inborn; they must be taught and learned as early as possible, starting in the nuclear family. Self-control comes through discipline. What we need back is sexual virtue. The one word for sexual virtue is *chastity*. It doesn't mean abstinence of sexual intercourse and pleasure but it includes it. It means *purity*: pure sex, right sex, not twisted sex. Since we are often tempted to kinky sex, chastity requires self-control, self-mastery. The heart is the seat where our feelings and acts originate: "For out of the heart come evil thoughts, murder, adultery, fornication, theft, false witness, slander." (Mt. 15:19). We need to become masters of our feelings and emotions again. There is nothing wrong with feeling attracted to other people, but when these feelings lead to infidelity, or acts of rape, prostitution, and pornography, things go seriously wrong.

The Catechism calls this "The Battle for Purity" (2520). Purity of heart brings freedom from widespread eroticism and avoids entertainment inclined to voyeurism and illusion

(2525). It is based on *modesty*, which guides how one looks at others and behaves toward them in conformity with the dignity of persons and their solidarity (2521); it protects the mystery of persons and their love (2522). Each one of us has to fight this battle for purity—and hopefully ends up winning. When the Catechism (1768) speaks of *passions*, it says that they are neither good nor evil, but they are "morally good when they contribute to a good action, evil in the opposite case." Sexuality is one of those passions; it needs to be curbed by rationality and morality. But that decision is up to us!

So the real issue for all parents is this: What does it mean to be a parent, as far as the Bible is concerned? The Bible makes no bones about it: Parents are the ones to pass on the Good News to the next generation—good news about God, about salvation, about "What we have heard and know; things our ancestors have recounted to us. We do not keep them from our children; we recount them to the next generation" (Ps. 78:3-4).

What makes parenting much harder nowadays is the fact that even parents who have created a healthy nuclear family cannot bring up children in a vacuum, for they are part of a society and have to live in a world dominated and indoctrinated by strong currents of relativism and secularism (see Chapter 1). Modern society doesn't make parenting easier. To counteract disruptive forces, parents have to become "activists" who bring identity back to their new generation. For example, more and more families practice home-schooling to avoid secular indoctrination in public schools. There are also attempts to start online high schools for Catholics. The Cardinal Newman Society has been very active in promoting and defending faithful Catholic education by developing K-12 education programs, and by advising parents and their children which colleges and universities to choose from a list of recommended Catholic colleges, for the term "Catholic" does not always stand for what it pretends to be.

Nevertheless, in spite of all that parents have done right, there are no families who haven't experienced pain and suffering—albeit to different degrees. All families are broken families. All families can find their brokenness exemplified in the Holy Family of Jesus, Mary, and Joseph. Don't be mistaken: the Holy Family was not the perfect, idyllic family many people imagine during the Christmas season and on Christmas cards. The picture of the Holy Family was far from rosy. Their child, Jesus, was born in a stable or cave, as there was no place for them in the inn. Joseph was a carpenter who had to work hard to make a living. Mary was told by Simeon that a sword would pierce her soul. The entire family had to flee to Egypt, like refugees, as Herod had put a price on the child's head. Soon Mary would become a widow at a rather young age. From then on, she had to take care of her two-person family without the welfare we know nowadays. Her son Jesus was condemned to death when he was only thirty-three years of age and was then executed in a cruel way, with his mother standing under his Cross. So Mary ended up as a lonely widow.

Could there be a more realistic picture of what family life can be like in this broken world? The Holy Family may not be the family we all dream of, and yet it is, because it is the family with which all broken families can identify, in some way or another. It is the kind of family Jesus wanted to become part of. That which made Jesus, Mary, and Joseph a Holy Family is the fact that they took all their sufferings as a blessing from God the Father. For us, that may not be so easy....

What we can learn from them is that we are supposed to hand on to the next generation the good things we have received ourselves. That doesn't alter the fact that parents can't give their children what they don't have themselves. How wise are the words of the Book of Sirach (48:10) when it says about the Prophet Elijah: "You are destined, it is written, in time to come to... turn back the hearts of parents toward their children." The comforting thought is that what we may not be able to do on our own, God can do for us.

4. A Broken Heart

An X-Ray of a Broken Heart

When we speak here about "the heart," we are not talking about an organ—something which can even be transplanted nowadays. In this book, "the heart" refers to our inner self. It is the heart that has reasons which reason doesn't know—in the words of Blaise Pascal. Most of us would probably agree that broken hearts find their origin in broken families, in broken generations, and in a broken world. But the reverse cause-and-effect relationship is probably equally true, or perhaps even more likely—that the brokenness of families, generations, and the world finds its origin in broken hearts.

Probably the main reason for a broken heart is suffering. We experience numerous kinds of suffering in life. There is *physical* suffering, such as catching an infection, having a genetic disease, growing a tumor, having a physical handicap, getting bodily injured, being hit by natural disasters. There is also *moral* suffering, such as being shot at, being lied to, going through a divorce, being abandoned, being persecuted, suffering sexual abuse, being bullied. We all have our own lists of physical and moral sufferings. People who do *not*, they just haven't lived long enough yet. We all have a cross to bear—our own individual cross, or actually our own personal crosses. Apparently, we are not alone in our brokenness but are part of a broken generation, even part of a broken world.

In addition, we also go through painful feelings. The heart is the seat where our feelings originate. As I said before, from feelings may come immoral desires, and from immoral desires may come immoral acts. There is nothing wrong with our feelings as such. We may not feel attracted towards certain people, but we cannot and should not actively reject them or hurt them. Although there is nothing wrong with our feelings, even if they are not "nice," we cannot ignore them, for when we suppress our feelings, they may come out in other ways—as violence, revenge, hate, murder, and the like. We cannot suppress feelings, but we do have the capacity and moral duty to suppress immoral acts. But once again, that requires self-control. We need to become masters of our feelings and emotions again. There is nothing wrong with feelings of hurt—everyone has them—but when they lead to acts of revenge, things go seriously wrong. Evil comes directly from acts, not from feelings.

Violence is often a consequence of feelings that were suppressed instead of being dealt with. It is a common misunderstanding that violence in intimate relationships usually comes from the male's side. Although men are more likely to injure their victims, women are more likely to use weapons to inflict harm, and frequently strike from behind or while their victim is sleeping. But other than that, there is not much difference between the sexes. Research has shown that, over the last twenty-five years, men and women commit violence at similar rates. In other words, violence in intimate relationships is not sex-specific. It is a deliberate act, often as a result of angry feelings that went out of control.

That's where self-control needs to come in, so we found out. Self-control can regulate how we act, not how we feel. About feelings there is no dispute. Feelings are not a good guideline for how to act. We are not in full control of our feelings, but we should at least try to be in control of our acts. We don't have to like all people, which is a matter of feelings—you like them or you don't—it only matters how we treat them. We all have friends and foes—people we like and people we don't like—but we should not treat our foes as foes. So it all starts in our hearts: "For out of the heart come evil thoughts, murder, adultery, fornication, theft, false witness, slander." (Mt. 15:19).

Again, feelings as such are not sinful, but acts can be. Feelings stay "inside," but it is acts based on those feelings that come out. It is acts, not feelings, that can have enormous direct consequences. We have to live with our wounded and broken feelings: the feelings of crime victims, of the divorced, of the parents hurt and rejected by their children, of the children neglected and mistreated by their parents. We have no control over those feelings; they come with living in a world that is broken. But what we do next with those feelings makes all the difference.

A good example of feelings is anger. For most people, anger has a bad name. But anger isn't necessarily bad—it's just a feeling. God can be angry (Ps. 38). Jesus was angry when he emptied the Temple (Mt. 21:12). Anger as such is not bad; it's a feeling not a sin. "Be angry but do not sin," said St. Paul (Eph. 4:26). Because of anger, we can either *under*react, and become depressed—or we can *over*react, so our anger gets out of control—many criminals are very angry people. There is nothing wrong with our angry feelings—everyone has them—but there may be something wrong with our behavior, the way we react to those angry feelings. More marriages and families today are dying from silence than from violence. A large percent of extra-marital affairs have some element of anger in them, as do many cases of divorce. The way we deal with anger is probably very similar to the way our parents did—it is handed down from generation to generation. We see it here again: broken families breed broken families with broken hearts.

If suffering is at the core of a broken heart, then the fundamental question is: How do we react to suffering? There are probably many different ways of how broken people deal with their broken hearts. The most common response to the suffering of a broken heart is to blame others. We blame our former wife or husband for a marital break-up, we blame our parents for the way we feel, we blame our teachers for our failing grades, we blame others when we are overweight or have become alcoholics, we blame people around us for giving us an infection. However, the most common candidate for being blamed is God. He has been blamed for everything we didn't like. I will get back to that later.

There are many afflictions in life that have broken our hearts. What is the problem of those afflictions? What all afflictions have in common is that they are distributed *unpredictably*: they strike the just as well as the unjust, believers as well as non-believers, the good and the bad alike. There seems to be no pattern. We all seem to have the same chances of being stricken by evil and suffering; no one is exempt; even one's religion does not seem to make a difference. Suffering could well be called the truest democratic experience of them all. In short, a broken heart is what we share with everyone else.

My second remark is that afflictions are distributed so *unequally*: some people have to stomach so much more than others. Some receive one blow after another, whereas others are apportioned meagerly. At times, we meet people who remain erect in a hurricane of misery; then again, we come across people who lament endlessly about trifles. Yes, we were created equal, but surely not as far as misery is concerned. Hearts can be broken in many ways and with various intensities.

All of this was well expressed by the Jesuit Claude la Colombière, who became a zealous promoter of the devotion to the Sacred Heart of Jesus:

> *All our life is sown with tiny thorns that produce in our hearts a thousand involuntary movements of hatred, envy, fear, impatience, a thousand little fleeting disappointments, a thousand slight worries, a thousand disturbances that momentarily alter our peace of soul. For example, a word escapes that should not have been spoken. Or someone says something that offends us. A child inconveniences you. A bore stops you. You don't like the weather. Your work is not going according to plan. A piece of furniture is broken. A dress is torn. I know that these are not occasions for practicing very heroic virtue. But they would definitely be enough to acquire it if we really wished to do so.*

But no matter how we turn it, we all end up having problems in life. They may differ in number, variety, and intensity, but the significant difference is how we deal with them. Some are overwhelmed by their problems and lose control over them, so they are controlled by their problems. Some are able to cope and manage their problems, because they took control of them. Some handle their problems so well that it looks like they have no problems at all. But that doesn't alter the fact that we all do have problems, even when we are able to hide them masterfully.

Loneliness is without doubt another part of a broken heart. It's arguably one of the most widespread diseases in this world. It affects everything in life: family life, school life, business life, neighborhood life. Mother Theresa calls loneliness and abandonment the worst disease in life. It is not only a disease that thrives in developmental countries, but it also prospers in highly developed environments, for it comes with broken families and wounded generations. It expresses itself in very diverse ways: violence, suicide, restlessness, attention deficit—and the list could go on and on. Those who are lonely and emotionally starved tend to search for alternatives to fill the void of loneliness with drugs, alcohol, and sex.

The late psychiatrist Viktor Frankl tells us that our understanding of life and suffering depends on the *meaning* we find in them: "If there is a why, then we can find a how." The real mental and emotional sickness many suffer from today is meaninglessness—not neurosis or psychosis. So the question is: How do we get meaning back in life? What I mean is boundless and bottomless meaning, not the superficial meaning we experience very often in life, at moments in which everything appears very meaningful to us. Those are merely moments when things are going our way or are simply going "well" for us—whatever that means. Yet when suffering hits us—sickness, terminal illness, accidents, disasters, catastrophes—we struggle. How can these things happen, we wonder, if life is supposed to be so meaningful? It is certainly a life-size question that calls for a life-saving answer.

How can we ever deal with such suffering? It is very tempting to give suffering a positive twist. That's often done by saying to people who lost their house, "Look not at what you do not have but at what you do have." Or by saying to people with a serious illness, "It could have been much worse," or "So many people have suffered worse things." Or by saying to a woman who lost her husband, "You still have your children." Or by saying to a disabled person, "Think of people who are not disabled but suffer so many other things." Or by saying to parents who cannot have children, "Don't forget children may also cause a lot of trouble." Or by saying to someone who suffers from being single, "Look at married people who are in trouble." Those are fake positive twists that deny, or at least ignore, that suffering is real. Sure, it is probably fair to say that everyone "dislikes" suffering, as something that should not be. But again, a dislike is a feeling; it becomes dangerous depending on how we deal with it. We cannot just make it disappear or talk it away. There must be better ways to deal with suffering.

A Cure for a Broken Heart?

Is there really a cure for broken hearts? Let's discuss first which therapies do *not* work. If you were to judge from the popular media, one of the most serious problems we have in our culture is the perceived lack of self-esteem. We just don't seem to value ourselves enough—at least that's what many believe.

Recently, Louise Hay, a self-help author, died. Imagine, one of her books sold 50 million copies. Here is a sampling of her "wisdom" (from her NYT obituary): "Every thought we think is creating our future"; "My happy thoughts help create my healthy body"; "Only good can come to me"; "I always work with and for wonderful people"; "In the infinity of life where I am, all is perfect, whole, and complete." No wonder McFerrin's song "Don't Worry, Be Happy" became so popular that it was a No. 1 U.S. pop hit in 1988 and won Song of the Year and Record of the Year honors at the 1989

Grammy Awards. But did it make our levels of anxiety and brokenness go down? Not that I noticed.

Like most advertisements, each one of these statements is basically a lie or half-truth, each one pretending to be worth millions of dollars. No wonder so many people want a piece of this self-help action. They are in search of a plan to improve self-esteem, self-worth, and feeling good about themselves. It's a tempting approach for those who think there is nothing "out there" or "up there," so they hope there is perhaps something meaningful "in there," deep in the most personal self. Searching for a "god within" has been tried in various ways: centering meditation, yoga, reiki, psychotherapy, up to and including the use of psychedelic drugs. Techniques like these may ease the pain temporarily, but certainly not in a lasting way.

Here is another fake cure. We have been told it's not fair when others hit the jackpot of life while we don't. So here is what you should do. Follow your dreams and demand your fair share of the pie. Demand what you want and when you want it, for you deserve it. Deflect attention from yourself and project your problems on others. Life isn't always wonderful, but *you* are. Trust yourself and insist you feel good about yourself. Here is your miracle cure: self-esteem—it is the best therapy in life to heal your broken heart! Really?

Something similar also holds for fighting loneliness. We live in a world in which loneliness is the most painful wound. We try to escape this loneliness with all kinds of techniques. The most popular one nowadays is psychotherapy. But loneliness remains with us as an inner emptiness. No matter how hard we try to fill this void, our high demands and expectations get constantly frustrated, because the truth is that no one can fill this void, not even a marriage partner or intimate friend.

Loneliness is something that does not disappear by getting married or joining a church group or starting some therapy. Social media don't help either. The more we get "connected," the more disconnected we turn out to be.

There must be something better than these inadequate therapies and cures. Well, I think there is. I would say the best therapy for a broken heart is to accept our brokenness and let suffering make us *better* instead of bitter. How can we possibly achieve this when we have no control over our sufferings?

The Bible tells us that it all began with the broken hearts of Adam and Eve, who refused to be "under God," but instead deemed themselves to be "next to God," or even "above God." That's how human brokenness came along. This moment in early human history is referred to as the Fall, which started the Original Sin. What does that mean? Well, think of this: If you come from a dysfunctional family, chances are you will start another dysfunctional family. We "inherited" a state of being "dysfunctional," so to speak. This idea mirrors the biblical principle that the sins of the fathers are visited onto the children to the third and fourth generations (Ex. 20:5; 34:6-7; Num. 14:18; Deut. 5:9).

There is probably no better term to capture this than "Original Sin"—it is not genetic, yet it is hereditary. C. S. Lewis even argued that the existence of Original Sin is perhaps one of the most obvious facts of human life, even so to non-believers. G. K. Chesterton called it "the only part of Christian theology which can really be proved." Indeed, you don't have to be a rocket scientist or a brain surgeon to know there is something fundamentally wrong with humanity, something that is "rotten" to the core. But the Bible tells us it's not God's doing, it's ours—and it goes back to the very beginning of humanity and has been around ever since.

Since the Fall, there is not only mental suffering—grief, hatred, frustration, heartbreak, guilt, humiliation, anxiety, loneliness, misery, self-pity—but also physical suffering—soreness, illness, disability, hunger, poverty, and ultimately death. All of these, and many other sufferings, cause broken hearts. No wonder Jesus says this about his mission, "[H]e has sent me to bind up the broken hearted" (Is. 61:1-2; cf. Lk 4:18-19). So if we ask ourselves the question, "Where does evil come from then?", then the shortest possible answer could be: from sin. Indeed, sin might very well be at the core of all evil (see Chapter 2).

Isn't "sin" a strange word in this context? It seems to be out of place here, as something coming out of the blue. Not really. As I said earlier, when a paralytic was brought to him, Jesus said, "your sins are forgiven" (Mk 2:5). The paralytic wanted to be released from his suffering and be able to walk—but certainly not to be delivered from his sins. Yet, Jesus saw the man's real need. Forgiveness of sins is the foundation of all true healing. Notice that Jesus does not offer us a cure for self-esteem; instead, he wants to save us from our sins.

What is "sin" then? Sin is any deliberate thought, word, or deed contrary to God's law. Sin is disobedience to God's law, thus God's will, thus God himself. The Catechism (1850) calls it "a revolt against God." Sin is the very *worst* there is, since it is the contrary of God who is the very *best* there is. "Sin" means more than "evil" or "vice." It is a specifically religious term. It means evil in its relation to God. It means damaging or breaking the relationship with God. The Catechism (386, 1850) explains:

> *Sin is present in human history; any attempt to ignore it or to give this dark reality other names would be futile. To try to understand what sin is, one must first recognize the profound relation of man to God, for only in this relationship is the evil of sin unmasked in its true identity as humanity's rejection of God and opposition to him, even as it continues to weigh heavy on human life and history.*
>
> *Sin sets itself against God's love for us and turns our hearts away from it. Like the first sin, it is disobedience, a revolt against God through the will to become "like gods," knowing and determining good and evil. Sin is thus "love of oneself even to contempt of God."*

As Bob Dylan used to sing, "Everything is broken. Broken bottles, broken plates, broken switches, broken gates, broken dishes, broken parts, streets are filled with broken hearts." That's the reality of life—at least on the surface. But there is another dimension to it. The Bible goes to a much deeper level, to the root of all brokenness in hearts, families, generations, and the entire world: sin. From Genesis 3 on, we live with the reality of Original Sin that permeates our entire lives, echoing across history and penetrating into every heart. In 1984, Pope John Paul wrote (in *Reconciliation and Penance*): "The restoration of a proper sense of sin is the first way of facing the grave spiritual crisis looming over man today."

Whereas the creation myths of many cultures hold that good and evil are inherent elements of human nature and the world order—it's supposedly the way things are and were made—Genesis corrects this error by revealing that evil is not rooted in creation but in humanity's abusive decision to turn away from God, from one another, and from God's created order through sin. Because of the Fall, the image of God has been corrupted, and Adam's sin has been passed on to the whole human race, which is called Original Sin. Although the goodness of their original creation remains, humans are now *flawed* images of God. Christianity is a religion of salvation. Salvation from what? From sin. If we had no sin, at least no sin deeply rooted in our nature, who would need Christianity? Who would need the suffering and death of Jesus?

The word "sin" is closely connected with the word "guilt." Should we feel guilty about certain things we did in life? Yes, definitely, for guilt is a fact of life. Our lives consist of failures, mistakes, and sins. Only a psychopathic person feels no remorse and claims not to experience any guilt. It is ridiculous to claim that we should never feel guilty. If that were true, we would live in a psychopathic society. Although there is indeed false guilt, there is certainly real guilt as well. Jesus helps people recognize their guilt by getting them to admit their sins. No wonder, the modern-day world tries to eliminate guilt by denying sin.

In order to admit sin, we need a conscience that makes us aware we have sinned. As we found out earlier, in the minds of many, the term "conscience" has become an empty label—a blank that we can fill with anything we want. It gives us a green light for anything we decide to do, for we are supposedly just following our conscience. For some enigmatic reason, the authority of a person's conscience still ranks high in the polls. Conscience is now the highest court of appeal—it has been given ultimate "primacy," coming close to infallibility.

Indeed, almost all people—Christian or not—have something about conscience that they respect, even if their theory is that it's nothing. So you wonder how this view can be so popular. The main reason probably is that the slogan "Follow your conscience" has become a permit for pursuing one's personal preferences, feelings, and desires. What has this idea led to? Well, when we follow this empty kind of conscience, we cannot really sin anymore. From then on, *anything* our conscience asks us to do is something morally good, and thus no longer a sin.

What is wrong with this interpretation? Let's use an analogy to explain what is wrong here. Our conscience has often been compared with technical devices we are all familiar with: a compass, a global positioning system (GPS), a barometer, an alarm, a gas gauge in a car, and the list goes on and on. These analogies are right about one thing: our conscience is indeed some kind of monitoring device—it monitors what is good or bad, right or wrong. But what they mask is that these devices are merely tools that may not work properly or may even fail entirely—and the same may be said about our conscience.

A real compass, for instance, functions as a pointer to the magnetic north because the magnetized needle typically aligns itself with the lines of the Earth's magnetic field—that is, with something outside itself. But it should not be used in proximity to ferrous metal objects or electromagnetic fields as these can affect their accuracy. At sea, for example, a ship's compass must be corrected for errors, called deviation, caused by iron and steel in its structure and equipment. Something similar holds for any kind of gauge. The gas gauge in your car may no longer go down because it is broken, yet the tank may be almost empty. And your GPS system may not work when something obstructs the connection with the satellite high above your head.

In other words, a person's conscience may indeed function in ways analogous to a compass or GPS, but these "monitoring" tools have to be monitored themselves and be aligned to an outside source—as does our conscience. Just as a compass needs to be aligned with the Earth's magnetic field and protected from surrounding interference, and a GPS system needs to be "aligned" to the right feed from satellites high in the sky, so needs a human conscience constant alignment too.

But also keep in mind that, because our moral compass can sometimes fail, it does not follow there is no right direction at all. Just like with math, we can get our sums wrong, but just because we disagree on some of the calculations, it doesn't follow that there is no right answer at all. So the question then is: What is the "right math" in morality? What is the right feed for our conscience? How do we properly align it? What do we align it to? In short, how do we calibrate our conscience?

The Catholic Church would say human beings were created with a moral compass pointing to, not the magnetic North, but the "Above"—to a place where justice reigns and moral laws reside. So, our conscience is not a private "compass" that determines its own North Pole. It has to be aligned to the one and only real "North Pole Above"—otherwise, we can easily go off track. So, obviously, there is more to it than having a conscience and following one's conscience. When people say, "Never disobey your own conscience," they forget one can do things "in good conscience," but also "with a bad conscience." So, a conscience on its own can be good as well as bad.

Besides, many don't even know they have a moral compass—or they don't use it, or it is defective—so they just follow their genitals in sexual affairs, or their curiosity in biomedical research, or their personal wishes in matters of life and death—no further questions asked. However, desires can't possibly be the source of morality, because it should be the other way around: morality judges our desires, not reversed. "Good" is not a matter of what *feels* good. Pleasure may feel good, but that doesn't automatically make it morally good. Following your feelings—which some mask as "following your conscience"—may sound nice, but more needs to be said.

In short, someone's conscience, let alone someone's feeling, cannot have absolute authority in and of itself. A person's conscience does not speak on its own but it merely reflects the moral laws bestowed on us by God. Our conscience does not create moral laws and values but merely receives them. That is the reason why we cannot take our conscience as an entirely private issue that we can form at our own discretion. One's moral judgment doesn't become true by the mere fact that it has its origin in conscience, because a conscience needs to be truthfully formed first so as to echo or reflect God's moral laws. To use our analogy again, a compass does not create its own magnetic field.

Therefore, a person's conscience is not the highest moral authority there is; it is subject to the supreme authority coming directly from God. As the Catechism (1776) puts it, "in the depths of his conscience, man detects a law which he does not impose upon himself, but which holds him to obedience.... His conscience is man's most secret core and his sanctuary. There he is alone with God whose voice echoes in his depths." So when people follow their conscience, it is important they listen to God's voice, not their own. When they don't, that's called sin.

We are all too familiar with the adage: "Hate the sin but love the sinner." This aphorism can easily leave the impression that our sins are floating out there totally independent of us. However, no sin can exist disconnected from a sinner. Sin and sinner are "intimately" connected. Yet, some like to modify that old saying as if it were saying "love the sinner so much that you don't bother mentioning the sin, for that would hurt the feelings of the dearly-loved sinner, and that would be a sin against Christian charity, wouldn't it?" Not really! And if you tell me that you do not see any sin because nothing is wrong in the world, I have a clear picture of what you are—that is, hopelessly naïve.

We know there is much suffering in this world. But what we should try to do in response is tracing our suffering back to sin instead of God. We are so used to blaming others for anything that goes wrong in life, and if we can't find anyone, we blame God. So it's not surprising then that many people ask how God can let all this suffering happen. They deflect the blame towards God. But here is the problem: Blaming God doesn't make us better; it makes us actually bitter. As a matter of fact, only God can heal our broken hearts, as long as we are willing to given him all the broken pieces.

How could we ever blame God for all evil in our world? Many people would say they have the right to blame him because God is all-powerful. Moral evil may be caused by humans, but what are we to do with physical evil? Physical evil is not our doing, so if it is someone's doing it must be God's doing. We discussed already (in Chapter 2) that physical evil can be traced back to moral evil, but this time we will focus on the idea some people have that evil must come from God because he is considered an all-powerful God.

The reasoning behind blaming God seems to be rather compelling: How does an all-powerful God get away with the evil in the world? The British philosopher David Hume, for instance, worded the problem as follows: “Is God willing to prevent evil, but not able? Then he is impotent. Is he able, but not willing? Then he is malevolent. Is he both able and willing? Whence then evil?” Objections like these have been made many times since and by many different people. If God is not able to take evil away, God cannot be all-powerful. And if God were really all-powerful, there should not be any physical evil. And yet there is!

What could be wrong with this kind of reasoning? Well, God is not almighty in the sense that he can do whatever he wants. For example, according to Thomas Aquinas, God is “limited” by his own reason—he cannot go against what is true and right, e.g. he cannot create square circles or undo something that happened in the past. Apparently, the omnipotent God has given part of his authority “away.” This is also very clear when it comes to *moral* evil. Moral evil is a consequence of the freedom God has given human beings. God could perhaps have chosen to eliminate the possibility of moral evil and evil-doing, but then God would have also taken away the possibility of good and doing-good—as well as the possibility of free choices.

It is clear that the possibility of moral evil is a consequence of this human freedom. How could God ever give us freedom without accepting its consequences up to the point of us freely choosing the wrong outcome? Human freedom is always a two-way street, leading us either *toward* God or *away* from God. So when God gave us freedom, he could not give us freedom without the potentiality for sin and doing evil. Therefore, evil can be, and must be, a very real consequence of human freedom. God can do so much good when we let him. And Satan can do so much evil when we let him. That’s why we repeatedly pray, “Thy will be done on earth as it is in heaven."

Something similar could be said about *physical* evil. God gave part of his authority "away" to the laws of nature which he implemented in this universe. Doesn't that mean, you might object, that the all-powerful God has become the victim of his own all-present laws? Not really! God could indeed have created a perfect world in which he was personally and directly in control of everything, but he decided not to. Instead, he made a world that runs on its own and is on its way to perfection. Aquinas says that it was in God's wisdom to ordain not to be responsible for all natural events. And it was also in God's wisdom to allow that there be "defects" in nature—such as a falling stone hitting your head or an earthquake destroying your home. Earthquakes and flu epidemics are not God's punishment but they are a consequence of the laws of nature.

Yet, the question remains how God could still allow such defects to happen? Here is the famous answer Aquinas gave us: if all evil were prevented, much good would be absent from the Universe; a lion, for instance, would cease to live if it could not kill its prey. In other words, whatever may be evil for the individual, the prey, is good for the larger picture, the Universe. Environmentalists are very aware of this fact; even "dangerous" animals such as venomous spiders and snakes play an essential role in their ecosystem; taking them out would disrupt the system. Or think of something like pain: we could be in real danger if there were no pain to alert us of harm. So God allows "defects" in secondary causes to exist because this contributes to the greater good of the whole so that the defect in one thing yields to the good of another, or even to the universal good.

Seen in this light, God's creation is in a state of journeying toward an ultimate perfection yet to be attained. The first chapter of the Book of Genesis calls God's creation "good," but it does not use the word "perfect." God's creation is not perfect yet, but it is on its way to perfection—and we human beings have been made participants in God's creation; we are his "co-workers" in bringing his creation to perfection.

In other words, God *wills* perfection but *allows* imperfection on the journey to perfection. So physical evil is part of the imperfection we are still surrounded by, and moral evil is a consequence of the Fall in Paradise. This makes the distinction between what God wills and what he allows even more important. Aquinas says that God "neither wills evils to be nor wills evils not to be; he wills to allow them to happen." God does not will earthquakes, but he allows them when they are a consequence of the laws of nature—in the same way as God does not will wars but allows them when humans use their freedom to start them. As a consequence, not everything that happens in this Universe is directly willed by God. To say that God "allows" or "permits" evil does not mean that he sanctions it in the sense that he approves of it, or even "wills" it, let alone directly causes it.

It is important to stress that God did not create evil, did not even want evil. Several Doctors of the Church, such as Augustine and Thomas Aquinas, have shown us that God did not create evil—certainly not moral evil, but not even physical evil. Evil is not like the things that the Creator created. God does not want evil—he wants and will good, but only allows evil. You might compare this with foods and drinks. If we don't eat or drink, we may suffer from hunger and thirst. But foods and drinks are not the cause of our hunger or thirst. It is a shortage of foods and drinks that cause those. In a similar way, evil is a *shortage* of good. For physical evil we have to blame the laws of nature; for moral evil we have to blame evildoers; and for sins we have to blame sinners—not God. What God created is good, but evil is the lack of the good God created and wanted.

These considerations should give us a different view of God. Instead of blaming God, we should change our ideas about the God we tend to blame for all that goes wrong—for that would make us only bitter, not better. Yet, it is quite understandable that we ask ourselves and God: Why is life so hard, and why should we thank God who allows life to be so hard? If we were God, then there wouldn't be so much suffering and evil, so we think. Yes, if we were God! But that pulls God down to the level of human beings. What is wrong then with human beings? The answer is rather simple, but direct: they are descendants of Adam and Eve who passed on to them the Original Sin.

Nevertheless, we are still left with the question of how to deal with the fact that God is Love. Whereas suffering may be as painful to Humanists, Marxists, Atheists, and Buddhists as it is to Jews and Christians, only the latter are haunted with this piercing question: "Why has God abandoned me?" Believing in a God of Love, believing in a good Creation, believing in the Providence of an all-loving God, causes the pain of suffering to penetrate to a deeper level—to the level of "Is something wrong between God and me?" The answer is, again, "Yes, sin!" Since the Fall, we are no longer "good" people who suffer "bad" things; instead, we are "bad" people who still enjoy so many "good" things. In other words, not only is there much good in the worst of us, but also much bad in the best of us. That's why we should never turn misery into self-pity.

Let me say it again, God does not want evil, but only allows evil—physical and moral. This may sound very un-Christian at first sight. When facing suffering and disaster, don't "pious" Christians love to say, "It's God's will"? They may even use such a line to hit people who were diagnosed with cancer or lost a child. They use it as an "aspirin" for all kinds of events ranging from a fire that kills a whole family to the death of the family dog. Instead, St. Paul says, "This is the will of God, your holiness: that you refrain from immorality" (1 Thess. 4:3). Instead of saying in times of disasters, "It's God's will," it is perhaps much better to say, "God will take care of it, in and through me. I must be an instrument of God's will. I am called upon to be God's hands and feet and arms now."

From now on, it doesn't make sense anymore to put the blame for evil on God's goodness, for hate on God's love, for errors on God's truthfulness. One cannot fight evil with more evil, hate with more hate, failure with more failures. Instead, we must fight evil with goodness, hate with love, failure with truth, and suffering with the Cross of Golgotha. It takes courage to not get discouraged. Some hurts we may never forget; wounds may heal, but scars often remain. With the help of Jesus we may be able to accept as he did and to forgive as he forgave. Only in this way can we become better instead of bitter.

This requires serenity—a feeling of peace without stress or anxiety—making us better instead of bitter. This is well expressed in the *Serenity Prayer* of Reinhold Niebuhr:

> *God grant me the serenity to accept the things I cannot change; courage to change the things I can; and wisdom to know the difference. Living one day at a time; enjoying one moment at a time; accepting hardships as the pathway to peace; taking, as He did, this sinful world as it is, not as I would have it; trusting that He will make*

> *all things right if I surrender to His Will; that I may be reasonably happy in this life and supremely happy with Him forever in the next. Amen.*

The only things we can change are ourselves. That's why all brokenness starts in the heart and then spreads from there to the family, to the generation, and ultimately to the world.

But serenity is not always easy to obtain. It is actually easier to nurse personal grievances. On Pearl Harbor Day, for instance, newspapers showed veterans well into their 90s with faces expressing the pain of grief as they remembered that fateful day way back in 1941. This made Fr. Jerry J. Pokorsky, a priest of the Diocese of Arlington.VA, remark:

> *There is the old joke about Irish Alzheimer's: you forget everything except your grudges. But it doesn't only affect the Irish. Anger is easy to understand – most of us know it all too well. It's there even in childhood. Take a rattle away from the baby, and he throws a temper tantrum. As we get older, we just get a bit more sophisticated in the way we express our anger – when others rattle us.*
>
> *If we aren't vigilant, it is quite possible for even petty anger to fester into true hatreds. We are quite capable of allowing a momentary annoyance to become the reason to nurse a grudge.*

5. A Broken Soul

An X-Ray of a Broken Soul

Perhaps, a broken soul cannot be "broken" in a literal sense, but at least souls can be stained. My soul, for instance, does have stains on it caused by what others did to me or by what I did to others. Even if we think we were never "stained," we still have an "original" stain on our souls that we "inherited" from our ancestors, going back to Adam and Eve. That's why each one of us has a broken soul, from the very moment we came into this broken world.

Where does this "soul" talk come from, you might ask. Well, it goes way back in human history. It is a rather technical issue, but let's just focus on the basics. The body is that part of us that we can see and feel—a part that will eventually die and turn back to dust. The soul, on the other hand, is something of us that we cannot see and that does not die. The soul may be hard to "capture," but it comes with an intellectual part, the *mind*, and a decision-making part, the *will*. Immoral acts are done with the body, but the immoral thoughts and decisions that they arise from come from the soul with its mind and its will. Body and soul are a two-some that we cannot easily deny. Those who deny the soul basically also deny that they have a mind and a will that is different from their body. Body and soul form a tight unity.

The Catholic Church has stressed this unity over and over

again. The Catechism (362 and 365) teaches us:

> *The human person, created in the image of God, is a being at once corporeal and spiritual.*
>
> *[I]t is because of its spiritual soul that the body made of matter becomes a living, human body; spirit and matter, in man, are not two natures united, but rather their union forms a single nature.*

It's rather unfortunate that this unity of body and soul has been compromised, especially by the philosopher René Descartes. He is seen as someone who separated the mind from the body, picturing the mind as "a pilot" in the "ship" of his body. We know this cannot quite be true. If it were true, the soul and mind would be aware of injuries to the body only at a distance—so the soul would understand them as a pilot perceives damage to his ship. That is not the way we are aware of our bodies. The body and the soul make for a "psycho-somatic" unity. In the Cartesian view, a pilot can be without a ship, and a ship can be without a pilot, so that damage to the ship does not directly damage the pilot. But in the Catholic view, there is no body without a soul. When the body hurts, the soul hurts, and when the soul hurts, the body hurts. Consequently, when the soul loves, the body loves. The soul loves through the body.

Yet, the idea Descartes promoted had at least two rather serious consequences. It gave some people more reason to think that the body is like a prison from which the soul wants to escape. It caused other people to do away entirely with Descartes' "pilot"—a ship without a pilot. These latter people still do accept the "body part" of a human person—which is indeed something almost impossible to deny—but they reject the "soul part" as something fictional and illusionary. But in so doing, I would say, they have lost an essential part of human life.

Why is it hard to believe that a human person has only a body but no soul? Since the mind is the intellectual part of the soul, we could also ask why is it hard to believe that a human person has only a brain, and no mind. It is hard to believe that the mind is identical to the brain—or the soul identical to the body, for that matter. Here are just a few reasons in a nutshell why the mind is more than the brain, so they cannot be one and the same thing.

First, whereas the brain as a material entity has characteristics such as length, width, height, and weight, the mind does not have any of those; thoughts coming from the mind are true or false, right or wrong, but never tall or short, heavy or light. Second, if the mind were just the brain, its thoughts would be as fragile as the molecules and neurons they supposedly came from, which makes all we claim to know, even in science, lose its very foundation. Third, although it is clear that we cannot understand anything without using our brains, it does not follow that our brains are doing the understanding. Think of this: when you use your eyes to count things, the counting is not done by the eyes but by the mind. The understanding is done by the mind that merely uses the brain and the eyes for its operations. Fourth, the very idea that thoughts are nothing but neurons firing in the brain would then also be nothing but neurons firing. This would make for a detrimental vicious circle—a kind of reasoning where you keep circling around, with no way to get in or out.

So if it is indeed true that the mind is different from the brain, yet is as real as the brain, we may have good reasons to also declare that the soul is different from the body, yet is as real as the body. If mind and brain are not identical, then soul and body are different from each other as well. Both sides of the equation appear to be equally *real*, which does not mean of course that both sides are equally visible or tangible. The body is material; the soul is immaterial.

We may conclude from this that it is vital to distinguish body and soul, as we do with mind and brain. The fact that we must distinguish them, however, does not mean that we can separate them, any more than the idea of a three-dimensional space means that we can separate those three dimensions from each other. Although we can mentally distinguish between our bodies and our souls, that does not make them divisible in practice. We can tell them apart but not set them apart. The fact that we can distinguish a flame's heat from its light, for instance, does not mean that we can separate the heat from the light. The same is true with body and soul. The body is always a person's body, and the soul is always a person's soul. We cannot isolate the soul from the body or take the soul out of the body. A body without a soul would be a corpse; a soul without a body would be something like a "ghost." A human being is therefore an incarnated soul as well as an animated body.

But wouldn't this also mean that the soul cannot exist on its own after death? No, it wouldn't. Here is why. Thomas Aquinas saw the soul as independent of the body in its existence, so it can "subsist," even after the dissolution of the body of which it is the "form." This means that the human soul has its being and its operation in itself, independent of anything else, including the body—for its intellectual acts are independent of any material organ. According to Aquinas, a human person is a material substance with an immaterial part, the soul, but this immaterial part is a substance in itself. What can operate independently must *exist* independently.

This idea of an independent soul, in spite of its connection with the body, may balance on the verge of contradiction, but it is not as strange as it sounds. Think of the analogy of language: We think with and through language, yet our thinking surpasses language and is not absorbed by it, in spite of our dependence on language. Dependence does not imply identity; dependence is one thing, identity quite another. In a similar way, although an embodied soul is fully tied to matter, it also surpasses matter and is not absorbed by it. Therefore, its capacity for immortality becomes a reality. It seems to make perfect sense that if the soul persists while the body keeps changing, the soul may also persist when the body is corrupted by death.

Although reason tells us humans are mortal—even if their souls are immortal—it is contrary to the nature of the soul to be deprived of the body. It is not a complete substance like for Descartes, but an incomplete substance (think of a heart that temporarily subsists on its own after taken from a donor). Consequently, says Aquinas, when separated from the body, the soul is in a "violent" state, and the desire of the immortal soul is to be joined again with its own body. This is not required by human nature as such, since by nature all humans are mortal—that is, with their death "they die," thus ending for a time the fullness of their personhood, namely the body-soul composite, even though their souls do not die—and therefore the resurrection of the body always remains a gratuitous gift of God to make the person whole again. When you die, your soul carries on, but you as a full person do not. However, the survival of your soul makes it possible for you as a person to live again, God willing. In other words, the soul is that part of us that lasts forever. In the resurrection, we do not become someone else other than the very same self once begotten and born into this world.

This is all in line with what the Catechism (366) teaches us:

> *The Church teaches that every spiritual soul is created immediately by God - it is not "produced" by the parents - and also that it is immortal: it does not perish when it separates from the body at death, and it will be reunited with the body at the final Resurrection.*

Nevertheless, death remains an impassible barrier: Human beings cannot conquer death even if they are able to escape it through their souls. After death, a separated soul does not depend on the body for its existence, but it is no longer a (full) *person*. In the words of the Catechism (1005),

> *To rise with Christ, we must die with Christ: we must "be away from the body and at home with the Lord." In that "departure" which is death the soul is separated from the body. It will be reunited with the body on the day of resurrection of the dead.*

Can we prove there is a soul? Proofs are surely possible in the world of mathematics, but souls are not a mathematical issue. Proofs are also possible in the world of science where experiments allow us to measure, weigh, quantify, and dissect things. But the soul is not something that can be dissected, measured, weighed, or quantified. To think differently fails to distinguish the immaterial soul from the material body. This failure made Duncan MacDougall, an early 20th-century physician in Haverhill, MA, measure how much mass a human body would lose when the soul departed the body upon death. He came up with a weight of 21 grams. A bizarre outcome! He mistook the soul for something material that can be weighed.

In other words, there are no scientific proofs that the soul exists. The best we have are philosophical arguments we discussed already. However, there are some empirical facts that make the existence of the soul (and its mind) very likely. One example comes from researchers at places such as the University of Virginia and the University of Vienna, Austria, who have been studying a phenomenon that is called "terminal lucidity"—the unexpected return of mental clarity and memory shortly before the death of patients suffering from severe mental disorders. It is the term used when dying people, who have previously been unresponsive or minimally responsive, suddenly gain clarity of mind for a few hours, often talking coherently with loved ones before passing away a short time later. Examples of this phenomenon include case reports of patients suffering from tumors, strokes, Alzheimer's disease, and schizophrenia. We know that there is no observable sudden change in the brain when death is very near. Is it possible, then, that the mind's sudden and short-lived return to normalcy just before death is brought about, not by some inexplicable surge in brain functioning, but by the soul's and mind's distancing themselves from the brain? Although terminal lucidity has been reported for around 250 years, it has received little scientific attention because of its complexity and transience—or perhaps because it goes against the now widely-held misconception that whatever the mind does is nothing more than what the brain does.

Even if this does not convince you that there is life-after-death—for the soul, and ultimately also for the body—you should at least think about the following. We don't know for sure what is behind that closed door of death until we have opened that door and have stepped through it. So should we really take the risk that life-after-death might be just an illusion? If the idea of life-after-death is true, it will be a gift from Heaven. If it is *not* true, we will never find out. This is what Blaise Pascal called his "wager," which he used more in specific for belief in God's existence, but which may also be appropriate to belief in life-after-death.

Peter Kreeft describes Pascal's Wager as follows: "If God does not exist, it does not matter how you wager, for there is nothing to win after death and nothing to lose after death. But if God does exist, your only chance of winning eternal happiness is to believe, and your only chance of losing it is to refuse to believe." In other words, atheism is a terrible bet, for it gives you no chance of winning. As Pascal put it, "If you gain, you gain all. If you lose, you lose nothing." Something similar might also hold for belief in life-after-death.

Put differently, at the end of life, a coin is being spun that will come down heads (life-after-death) or tails (no life-after-death). How will you wager? When Blaise Pascal introduced his *Wager*, he was trying to show that *not* to wager is an impossible option. The reason is simple, in the words of Peter Kreeft: "Because we are moving. The ship of life is moving along the waters of time, and there comes a point of no return, when our fuel runs out, when it is too late. The Wager works because of the fact of death." So each one of us has no choice but to wager in the face of death, given the possibility that we might be judged by God after death. By "sitting on the fence," we actually wager *against* God. It could be said that by refusing to choose, one has already chosen to wager on the idea that picking no belief is safer than accepting a false belief—which could be a pretty dangerous bet.

This may look like a very cold, analytical approach that does not really touch our hearts or souls, but it does tell us how important it is to make the right choice at the end of life—or even during. As C. S. Lewis put it, those "who did most for the present world were just those who thought most of the next." We're constantly reminded: *Memento mori*, remember that you will die—and therefore be prepared. That's very good advice, not only because it puts other things about life and death in the proper perspective, but also because it's literally true that any day may be your, my, anybody's last. Yet, among the many things we've lost in the breakdown of Catholic culture in the last half-century is attention to the most important end-of-life-question: how to die.

This is what Cardinal Bellarmine said, four centuries ago, about the end-of-life and the "art" of dying:

> *Now everyone will admit, that the "Art of dying Well" is the most important of all sciences; at least everyone who seriously reflects, how after death we shall have to give an account to God of everything we did, spoke, or thought of, during our whole life, even of every idle word; and that the devil being our accuser, our conscience a witness, and God the Judge, a sentence of happiness or misery everlasting awaits us.*

No matter how we turn it, there is something very paradoxical in how we deal with life and death issues: we fear death, and at the same time we fear life. For people who do not understand the world they live in, life as well as death are loaded with fear. There seems to be fear of death as well as fear of life in this broken world.

One the one hand, there is this unrelenting fear about *death*. This is understandable, for it is very normal to experience great anguish at the thought of death. That fear is even amplified by the fear that we have to give up the joys of life.

This latter fear has led to a booming industry of developing the long-awaited miracle drug that prolongs life, perhaps even indefinitely. We make every effort possible to rejuvenate ourselves with medical interventions, such as plastic and cosmetic surgery, or chemical substances, such as hormones and steroids. And when death seems to be near, we do everything possible to keep ourselves and others alive with the most advanced tools at our avail.

Recently, the power of medical technology has become greater than ever before. Decades ago, doctors made full use of the little bit they happened to know to prevent us from dying. Nowadays, doctors use everything that they have come to know to keep us alive. They are able to rejuvenate us, to relieve pain with medication, to destruct our cancers, to artificially feed us, to connect us to a ventilator, and to resuscitate us. We feverishly try to delay death to keep the joys of life going and the fear of death at bay.

But no matter how hard we try to delay death, death is in everyone's future. A close friend of St. Thomas More used to keep a skull on his dinner table to remind himself that death is in our future. Medical experts even tell us that, if we lived long enough, sooner or later we would all eventually die of cancer. But it is hard, if not impossible, for doctors to predict at exactly what time you will die. When a physician tells you that you have only six more months to live, don't take that as an exact scientific statement; scientists cannot even accurately predict tomorrow's weather. And besides, there is always God!

On the other hand, not only do we fear death, but there is also this fear about *life*: we don't want to live any longer with the pains of a broken heart. This makes some people wish they could just terminate their painful and broken lives.

Sometimes this even leads to the actual decision of terminating painful lives—either through suicide or through euthanasia. The idea behind this is that I have the right to make a decision about my own body—either to live or to die—for it is "my" body.

In this context, Pope John Paul II has drawn attention to the two radically different meanings of the word "my." When I say, "This is my cell phone," I mean that I *own* the phone. On the other hand, when I say, "This is my wife," it is clear that I am not claiming that I own her, but that I am *part* of her. So what do we say when someone says "This is *my* body, therefore I can do with it as I please"? We are so hung up on possessions that we view even personhood in terms of ownership, saying that we *possess* our bodies. However, if a human being consists of both soul and body, I cannot say that a person "has" a body. If you still do want to use ownership terminology and want to say you "have" a body, then you must add that you also "have" a soul with a mind and a will.

The erroneous idea that I own my own body, and therefore can do with it whatever I decide, has become very prevalent these days. In a sense, it's true that my body is *my* body, something I own, for I can control the use of my arm, for instance, by choosing to swing my arm. But as we said earlier, we do not *have* a body, we *are* a body in the sense that our soul forms it. In that particular sense, as well, our body is not some kind of machine that we own. It is "my" body but not "mine." If there is anyone who owns my body, it is the one who made it, God. Therefore, I am not allowed to sell or kill my own body—that's a decision beyond my authority. Mary Eberstadt calls it "ironic that a popular movement known by the slogan 'keep your rules off my body' has no trouble telling other people what to do with theirs."

Yet, that's what happens in cases of abortion, suicide, and euthanasia: we take life and death in our own hands. This is most obvious in suicide, but it also happens in euthanasia, especially in what is euphemistically called physician-assisted suicide. Expressed as "physician-assisted suicide," it sounds so reasonable. But what exactly is reasonable about self-destruction? Euthanasia is based on the assumption that certain people will be better served by being dead—a dubious premise indeed, as Cardinal Seán O'Malley rightly pointed out. Not only is the term "doctor-assisted suicide" confusing—for how can it be suicide if it is assisted?—but it is also misleading, as the only "assistance" the patient receives from the doctor is a prescription to be filled at a pharmacy. Therefore, a more realistic and accurate description of "doctor-assisted suicide" would be "doctor-prescribed death."

This form of euthanasia has been defined by Pope John Paul II, in his encyclical *Evangelium Vitae*, as "an action or omission which of itself and by intention causes death, with the purpose of eliminating all suffering." The pontiff explicitly adds that "euthanasia is a grave violation of the law of God, since it is the deliberate and morally unacceptable killing of a human person." Some people justify active euthanasia, or physician-assisted suicide, on the grounds that the pain of terminal illness is too great for the average person to bear. They hold that it is more merciful to kill suffering patients than to keep them alive. They cleverly swap one moral value, the sanctity of life, with another moral value, the prevention of suffering.

Here is a chilling account of what this may lead to. In July of 2016, Betsy Davis sent an e-mail to her closest friends and relatives: an invitation to a two-day party at a beautiful house in Ojai, California. But this was not going to be your usual party, she explained: at the conclusion of the celebration, she was going to end her own life with a lethal combination of drugs provided by her physician to end her suffering. Really, ending her suffering? How do we know that Betsy's suicide ended her suffering? To be sure, we can observe that the current form of suffering from physical illness has ended for her, but how do we know what happened after the death of her body? Her suffering may be carried over to Hell. Her physician-assisted suicide brings us to the cliff of a new version of Pascal's wager: Are we going to take the chance, with no supporting evidence, that suicide ends all our suffering? Instead, we may end up in Hell. Is it worth the "risk" that maybe there is more than our present suffering? By deciding what she did, Betsy had already lost her wager.

Seen in the light of what we have discovered so far, we must come to the conclusion that broken hearts die when our bodies die, but—and that's the salient point—broken souls do *not* die. Some still think we can "heal" broken hearts by bringing an end to life—for instance, through suicide or euthanasia—but that only kills the body, or at best a broken heart, but not a broken soul. Obviously, people who deny there is a soul in each one of us will insist killing the body ends life completely and definitely. A faithless view makes us believe that suffering stops at the grave. There is this gravestone of an atheist in the town of Thurmont, MD, that I think could not express things better: "Here lies an Atheist. All dressed up and no place to go."

But the truth is quite different: to hold that suicide and doctor-assisted suicide end all suffering is to depart from reason and science, and to take a leap of blind faith based on the power of one's own speculation about what happens after the death of the body. As a matter of fact, no higher authority has revealed to us that any form of suicide ends all suffering. There might very well be more to us than a body—a soul, that is!

The issue of life and death draws us once more back to that momentous moment of the Fall in Paradise. The core issue here is that all of us have a broken, tainted soul. I know it is a well-known account of what happened in Paradise, but let's look closer at the outcome of the Fall in Genesis 3:17-19, 23:

> *Cursed is the ground because of you! In toil you shall eat its yield all the days of your life. Thorns and thistles it shall bear for you, and you shall eat the grass of the field. By the sweat of your brow you shall eat bread, Until you return to the ground, from which you were taken; For you are dust, and to dust you shall return.... The Lord God therefore banished him from the garden of Eden, to till the ground from which he had been taken.*

It is a devastating description in a nutshell of a broken world with broken hearts, broken families, broken generations, and ultimately broken souls. From then on, each one of us would be destined to die, in spite of the fact that we were originally created with immortality. But fortunately we have more than a body: a soul!

Before the Fall, we are told, Adam and Eve were preserved from death and suffering: "The Lord God gave the man this order: 'You are free to eat from any of the trees of the garden except the tree of knowledge of good and evil. From that tree you shall not eat; when you eat from it you shall *die*'" (Gen 2: 16-17). What this means is explained by the Catechism (396, 400) as follows:

> *The "tree of the knowledge of good and evil"*

> *symbolically evokes the insurmountable limits that man, being a creature, must freely recognize and respect with trust. Man is dependent on his Creator, and subject to the laws of creation and to the moral norms that govern the use of freedom.*
>
> *The harmony in which they had found themselves, thanks to original justice, is now destroyed: the control of the soul's spiritual faculties over the body is shattered; the union of man and woman becomes subject to tensions, their relations henceforth marked by lust and domination. Harmony with creation is broken: visible creation has become alien and hostile to man. Because of man, creation is now subject "to its bondage to decay". Finally, the consequence explicitly foretold for this disobedience will come true: man will "return to the ground", for out of it he was taken. Death makes its entrance into human history.*

How did Adam and Eve know what their future death would be like, given the fact that they were created immortal? Was there death before the Fall? The Book of Genesis seems to assume there was. As a matter of fact, carnivores were created with organs expressly intended for causing the death of other animals. When God threatened Adam and Eve with death for disobedience, the Bible seems to imply they had some knowledge of what death is, as they had seen it among animals. So after the Fall, we ended up with a paradoxical situation: fear of life as well as fear of death.

Although the material world is indeed subject to decay and death, humans are not, because they have been endowed with an immortal soul. For an immortal soul, prior to sin, the death of the body would be a punishment undeserved. Adam and Eve were created for immortality, but then lost the eternal life of the soul in the moment they sinned, and physically died many years later. After the General Resurrection, God will restore to us the grace needed to prevent our bodies from breaking down permanently. As St. Paul says, "[T]hrough one person sin entered the world, and through sin, death, and thus death came to all, inasmuch as all sinned" (Rom. 5:12). Thus St. Paul contrasts the universality of sin and death with the universality of redemption in Christ.

A Cure for a Broken Soul?

How can a broken soul be healed? The soul connects us directly to God, whom we may have offended. Each offense toward God puts another stain on the soul. Since the soul gets stained by sin, the cure for a broken soul can be caught in one word: *repentance*—in hope of God's forgiveness for our sins.

Of course, repentance doesn't make much sense if there is no God. Without God, there wouldn't be broken souls either—only broken hearts at best. The word "repentance" just does not exist in the vocabulary of atheists. Atheism has a tolerant and an intolerant version. The former version is found in the person who says, "I myself don't believe in God, but you, feel free to believe God exists." Intolerant atheists, by contrast, flatly deny that God exists, and they make it very clear that you, too, should not believe in the existence of God, for the same reason that you should not believe in elves and fairies—because there are no such things. That's why repentance is completely out of the question for atheists, tolerant or intolerant.

I am not planning to counteract either kind of atheism. Let me just say this. If God is Existence and Being in itself, then the question "Does God exist?" is the same as asking "Does existence exist?" or "Does being exist?" The only reasonable answer to that kind of questions is, "Of course!" God is existence, and existence *exists*! God is being, and being *is*! Nothing comes from nothing by nothing, as the saying goes—not even the universe. So there must be something that causes the universe to exist. There must be something that is "behind" anything else and "higher" than anything else. It doesn't make sense for atheists to claim that nothing is the highest something, for "nothing" just means "not something." Does that line of reasoning make for a scientific proof of God's existence? Probably not. However, no matter how strong the empirical and rational evidence is in favor of God's existence, most atheists *choose* not to accept God's existence as a fact because they don't like the way the world looks to them with God in the picture. So, proof doesn't really matter to them.

God cannot be "proven" in a scientific way. No matter what "proof" we come up with, we should not forget what Thomas Aquinas, the mastermind behind the "proofs" of God's existence, remarked: "To one who has faith, no explanation is necessary. To one without faith, no explanation is possible." Atheists typically reject any explanation. They live their lives as if there is no God: they don't say prayers, they don't go to church (except for weddings and funerals perhaps), and they certainly don't regard the rules of morality as God-made commandments. Without God, there wouldn't be sin, either. If there is no sin, repentance would also be out of the question. And without sin, there wouldn't be broken, tainted souls, and we wouldn't need repentance.

However, reality is that no one is without sin. The Bible keeps repeating this over and over again. "If we say, 'We are without sin,' we deceive ourselves, and the truth is not in us" (1 John 1:8). Or, "[T]hey are all under the domination of sin, as it is written: ‘There is no one just, not one’” (Rom. 3:10). Or, “[A]ll have sinned and are deprived of the glory of God” (Rom. 3:23). Because of this, each one of us has a broken, tainted soul that is in need of repentance for the sins that have tainted our souls. On the other hand, how “obvious” is it that we need to *ask* for forgiveness, you might ask. Isn’t there also God’s eternal mercy which takes all our stains away without us even asking for it? Isn’t repentance redundant if there is infinite forgiveness?

Behind these questions is the erroneous idea that God’s mercy and forgiveness are like a blank permit for whatever we do wrong. The problem is that the word “mercy” can easily be misunderstood. “Lord, have mercy” does not translate into “God, go easy on me.” Mercy does not mean to be “soft on crime.” Mercy does not wipe out sin and evil on the press of a button. Why not? Well, there are at least two reasons.

The first reason why God cannot just ignore our sins is that he would basically ignore the freedom he had bestowed on us when he created us in his image and likeness. God takes us seriously. Ignoring our sins would violate our integrity as human beings. He could not just ignore the freedom he had given Adam and Eve in Paradise when they went against his commandments. Their choice against God called for “action” on God’s part: they were removed from Paradise. Committing sin inevitably has grave consequences that cannot be just blotted out.

The truth is this: Because we are free human beings, we will be held accountable for all the choices we make in life. Evil is a matter of bad choices, and bad choices affect not only our own lives, but also those of others. Moral evil is very real, as we saw earlier, so our sins that caused moral evil are very real too—they cannot just be ignored. If God would ignore them, our human freedom would amount to nothing. God could perhaps have chosen to eliminate the possibility of evil and evil-doing, but then God would have also taken away the possibility of good and doing-good—as well as the possibility of free choices. God has given human beings the freedom to act for or against him, so God acts through persuasion, not by coercion.

It is obvious that the possibility of moral evil is a consequence of this human freedom. How could God ever give us freedom without accepting its consequences up to the point of us freely choosing the wrong outcome? So when God gave us freedom, he could not give us freedom without the potentiality for sin and doing evil—that would be logically contradictory. Therefore, moral evil can be, and must be, a very real consequence of human freedom. Unlike dictators who take human freedom away, God made us in his image and thus he created us, not as marionettes, but as beings endowed with freedom as well.

As a matter of fact, human freedom would remain hanging in the air if there were no God. We have nothing to base it on, other than God. It certainly cannot be based on genetics. If genes would determine the outcome of our choices, then we cannot really make free choices and have basically lost the free will we thought we had. If we want to claim human freedom, then we need someone from whom this freedom derives—a Creator God. How could there be human freedom if there were no God who has freely created us after his image? In Paradise, he gave us human freedom as a reflection of his divine freedom. Therefore, God takes our choices and actions seriously, also when they are evil and call for repentance.

Another reason why God cannot just ignore our sins is that God is not only *merciful*—which might indeed lead to unconditional forgiveness—but he is also *just*—which cannot ignore what we did wrong. Mercy and Justice go hand in hand in God's Kingdom. To go "soft" on sin may sound merciful, but it would violate justice at the same time. God is Infinite Goodness and Love, which includes his Mercy as well as his Justice—for he is a God of Mercy as well as a God of Justice.

These are the two keywords that characterize how God deals with us: Mercy *and* Justice. This twosome should not be hard to understand. Good parents are fair towards their children when they use justice, but they are also forgiving when they see remorse and use mercy. There is a delicate balance between the two. Something similar can be said about God. There is indeed God's Mercy, but not unconditionally, for he is also a God of Justice. His just actions are merciful, and his merciful actions are just—similar to the way parents sometimes have to punish their child out of love.

Like in court, justice means that the verdict can be either conviction or acquittal. In the case of God's justice, there can be salvation as well as damnation, so that both his Mercy and his Justice might be more perfectly manifested—neither one without the other. *Mercy* may lead us to salvation, whereas *justice* may lead us to damnation. God's mercy and his justice go hand in hand. Therefore, St. Augustine advises us, "After sin, hope for mercy; before sin, fear justice."

True, there is God's infinite mercy, but mercy does not wipe out all moral evil automatically or automagically. It requires some action on our side—to repent and to ask for forgiveness. We need to acknowledge first what we did wrong. Mary's *Magnificat* proclaims this very clearly: "His mercy is from age to age," but it emphatically adds, "to those who fear him" (Lk. 1:50). It is certainly important to mention God's mercy. But this information could easily obscure that justice demands from us that we must first acknowledge that we sinned and did what is wrong in God's eyes. So, mercy does not automatically wipe out all the evil we caused, but only the evil that we ask forgiveness for. God's mercy is boundless, but to access it requires repentance. As Fr. James Schall, S.J. puts it, "Mercy without judgment bypasses free will."

St. Paul, for instance, makes no bones about it. Paul was a realist. In long-ago Galatia—but it could be anywhere else—he found "immorality, impurity, licentiousness, idolatry, sorcery, hatred, rivalry, jealousy, outbursts of fury, acts of selfishness, dissension, factions, occasions of envy, drinking bouts, orgies, and the like" (Gal 5:19-21). And then he speaks of the consequences: "Those who do such things will not inherit the Kingdom of God." He knew very well that people do such things, often even frequently. Christianity is initially presented to us because we are sinners who "do such things." But if we do such things, says St. Paul, then we will not inherit the Kingdom of God—unless... Unless we repent and ask for God's forgiveness.

What is hard to accept for many people is the fact that some of us will undergo salvation but others damnation, depending on what we have done or not done in life. In the minds of many, that seems to go against a loving God who is full of mercy. But, again, then they forget God is also a God of justice who cannot ignore that through our own free actions we may call either salvation or damnation upon ourselves. Salvation is God's choice, of course, but God's choices are based on our choices. As St. Augustine put it, God "did not will to save us without us."

From this follows conclusively that the ultimate consequence of human freedom is the existence of an eternal Heaven as well as an eternal Hell, the existence of eternal salvation as well as eternal damnation. Certainly no sane person wants Hell to exist, just as no sane person wants evil to exist. But evil does exist. If there is a free will, then there must be evil; if evil and eternity exist, then there must be Hell. Hell is merely evil eternalized. C. S. Lewis called Hell "the greatest monument to human freedom." The Catechism (1861) puts it this way: "Our freedom has the power to make choices for ever, with no turning back."

Besides, there is another reason why there is the salvation of an eternal Heaven as well as the damnation of an eternal Hell: there is too much injustice left in a broken world. There is this huge amount of injustice that God's Justice must set straight. Think of this: many have died or will die without ever having been welcomed into life, without ever having received love, comfort, or even justice from their fellow people. Some of us experience lots of rejection, violence, poverty, suffering, pain, and injustice. Some of us may not have had much to live for. This is the reality of broken souls, which calls for a Last Judgment, as mentioned in the Bible.

As a matter of fact, a final judgment is the answer to many questions we may have in life. What about all those people who have experienced so little joy in their lives, or who suffered so many tragedies? What about all those victims of infertility, abortion, eugenics, and euthanasia? What about all those victims of genocide, gas chambers, torture dungeons, terrorism, wars, drugs? What about all those people who cannot be called back to life to receive a bit more warmth and love here? What about those who were neglected by their spouses, their parents, or their children? So many people had hoped for something good but were given so much evil and suffering instead. What are we to do with all of these people?

Put differently, there are many "debit" accounts that still need to be settled—not so much those little accounts that one might like to settle with one's neighbors, but rather those enormous accounts that caused immense sorrow, pain, and disaster to millions of people. The fact that we speak in terms of "accounts that need to be settled" implies already that we can go up "into Heaven" to see everything dimly from God's perspective. That is what a final judgment is about. All those "debit" accounts need to be settled, even after death.

If there were no final judgment, those accounts would remain unsettled. In a God-less world, there is no hope that those issues would ever be addressed. Yet, the earth is crying out for justice! If there is no instant repayment for good or bad actions and choices, there must be a final repayment in the final-final stage of life. We need and deserve to be judged, if God is also a Just God. Good actions God can reward with Heaven, bad ones with Hell. God does not judge us on our feelings and emotions, for those are sometimes beyond our control, but he does judge us on our actions, on our free choices in life.

But you might ask: what about Jesus' Crucifixion, which we are told redeemed everyone? You are right: *Redemption* is indeed for all, because Christ "died for all," in the words of St. Paul (2 Cor. 5:15). The Catechism (605) puts it very emphatically, "There is not, never has been, and never will be a single human being for whom Christ did not suffer." After it had been closed since the Fall, Heaven was opened again for us through Jesus' redemption on the Cross—yes, opened for all of us. However, redemption is not the same as salvation. *Salvation* results from repentance, from accepting Jesus' redemption and living one's life accordingly. But those who do not accept this gift of universal redemption—unless it is "through no fault of their own"—may still miss out on salvation and may not end up in Heaven. Although redemption is universal, salvation is not. The Catechism (55) makes it very clear that God gave us "the hope of salvation, by promising redemption." Redemption has opened Heaven for all, but that does not mean that all will in fact go to Heaven.

Yes, God's forgiveness exists, but again, not unconditionally. Pope Benedict XVI put it this way: Unconditional forgiveness—the abolition of Hell—would be a kind of "cheap grace" to which the German Protestant theologian Dietrich Bonhoeffer rightly objected in the face of the appalling evil that he encountered in Nazi Germany in his day. If God does not will to save us without us, then there must be not only salvation, but also damnation. If there is eternal salvation, there must also be eternal damnation. We cannot blame God for this because people who commit grave evil condemn themselves. God does not save those who do not want to be saved. Hell is a state of "definitive self-exclusion from communion with God," according to the Catechism (1033). The afterlife—life-after-death—makes for a period of repayment—for the good things done as well as the bad things done.

We end up with a very uncompromising black-and-white picture—either eternal salvation or eternal damnation. Fortunately, says the Catholic Church, there is also something in between Heaven and Hell, a kind of "middle state" called *Purgatory*. It is a place or condition of temporal punishment for those who depart this life in God's grace. The

Catechism (1030) says about Purgatory: "All who die in God's grace and friendship, but still imperfectly purified... undergo purification, so as to achieve the holiness necessary to enter the joy of heaven." What does this mean? I think this is best explained by an example the late and legendary Mother Angelica of EWTN once used: If a prostitute had a profound conversion and decides to enter Mother Angelica's convent, a one-day transition would definitely be too short a period for such a person to make the transition—actually a massive shock—in spite of all her good intentions. Indeed, for most of us, the transition from a life on earth to a life in Heaven would be equally dramatic, actually so shocking that we would need some extra preparation time, as nothing unclean can enter the presence of God, according to the Book of Revelation (21:27).

As the late Fr. Benedict Groeschel put it, "Purgatory is not a temporary hell, but a preliminary heaven." It is a place or state where human imperfection is corrected in the "fire of *purification*" before we can enter God's Heaven where nothing unclean shall enter. The idea of purification is counter to the cheap optimism that prevails nowadays in the minds of many, holding that the life of practically everybody automatically ends up in a state of bliss. However, the truth is that not everybody's life ends up in a state of ecstasy. Since we all have stained souls, the only way to remove such stains is repentance and remorse.

When we do some self-examination, we readily admit how often we conceal from ourselves our greed, lust, selfishness—all the deadly sins that stain and break our souls. They are sometimes hiding in the recesses of our souls. Who does *not* have skeletons in the closet? However, Catholics believe that the remedy lies in the proven paths of repentance, conversion, and grace. The blind man said to Jesus, "Jesus, have pity on me" (Lk. 18:38). Each one of us should repeat this, for all of us are *pitiful* people. We are as broken and wounded as the blind man was. We need to ask Jesus to have pity on our broken souls, for broken they are. When the Prophet Isaiah (61:1) says, "He has sent me to bring good news to the afflicted, to bind up the brokenhearted," we should realize that each one of us needs to hear that good news since we are all broken and in need of repentance and forgiveness.

An old Chassidic parable tells us about a fool who has a rude awakening when he arrives at the Heavenly Court after his years on earth. "God [Hashem] gave you a gorgeous house," says the Heavenly Tribunal. "Who, me?" replies the fool. "I never owned my own house—I rented." "We're not talking about the wood and stone dwelling," says the Heavenly Tribunal. "We're referring to the exquisite edifice that housed your soul. You ruined it with what you did. You failed to perform the required maintenance on it. You never thanked God for the trillions of miracles he did for your 'house' every day, and you never repented the damage you did to your soul. You received more than a beautiful house—God gave you a home!"

However, this beautiful home, the human soul, is actually a battlefield where a cosmic war is being waged. There is a cosmic warfare going on, so to speak, between Good and Evil, between God and Satan. It is God's aim for each one of us to attain Heaven after death, whereas Satan's aim is to ensure that as many people as possible miss that eternal goal and end up in Hell. We should never forget that the question "How real is evil?" runs parallel with the question "How real is Satan?" The Catholic Church doesn't want us to forget that Satan is a real force with whom to reckon. If there is no Satan, then the Cross is a hoax; if there is no Satan, then the whole economy of salvation is up for grabs. No wonder Christianity sees the history of humanity as a perpetual, cosmic warfare between God and Lucifer, between good and evil, between the Light of God and the darkness of evil, between God calling us to be like His image and Satan enticing us to be our own image, which is Satan's image.

Satan is real! It is the power of Satan that enabled men such as Hitler, Stalin, and Mao to spellbind and enslave the minds and spirits of millions, creating hell ahead of time, right here on earth. This explains how such people have sold their souls by following "orders" that stem from sources far beyond their own resources. Some satanic force engaged in a battle against God's creation gave them more than mere human power. The Catechism (2851) makes it very clear, "[E]vil is not an abstraction, but refers to a person, Satan, the Evil One, the angel who opposes God."

Not only does this cosmic warfare occur on the large scale of history, but it also rages on the small scale of our inner self where decisions are being made *for* or *against* God. Satan works day and night on the personal battlefield of our souls. The fuel behind all our sins is some satanic force engaged in a battle against God's creation—which is the role of Satan, the "father" of all lies, the great divider who knows how to remain hidden behind the scene. Satan is happy to lend us some "spiritual" help to do whatever is against God's commandments. Prayer is the best weapon in this battle. Satan is in constant communication with our souls, if we let him. This is even more dangerous when we are unaware of the battle that is taking place in our souls. That's why Satan loves to hide or disguise himself. To deny he even exists is one of Satan's best ploys.

Let's make clear, though, that Satan is not the opposite of

God—an anti-god. According to the Bible, Satan is a created being, having been created by God as His most powerful angelic helper. So, Satan is an angel who rebelled against God. He continues to prowl the earth like a ravenous, roaring lion "looking for someone to devour" (2 Pet. 5:8). Satan and the other evil spirits prowl about the world for the ruin of souls.

Archbishop Fulton Sheen provided us with a keen insight into Satan:

> *Do not mock the Gospels and say there is no Satan. Evil is too real in the world to say that. Do not say the idea of Satan is dead and gone. Satan never gains so many cohorts, as when, in his shrewdness, he spreads the rumor that he is long since dead. Do not reject the Gospel because it says the Savior was tempted. Satan always tempts the pure—the others are already his.*

Each time we do side with Satan—that is, against God—we add another stain to our souls. This raises the question of how we can get rid of those stains. St. Augustine tells the famous story of how he stole pears from an orchard as a child. Then he astutely remarked about his stealing, "I had no wish to enjoy what I tried to get by theft; all my enjoyment was in the theft itself and in the sin." Don't just stare at the odd example St. Augustine uses. It happens all the time. Some lie frequently just for the mere enjoyment of the lie itself. Some use guns just for the mere enjoyment of killing in itself. Some bully others just out of pure enjoyment. Some ridicule the religious beliefs of others just for the pleasure it gives them. And the list goes on and on. The sin itself gives them enjoyment.

These are examples of the perverse will that chooses evil for its own sake—a consequence of Original Sin in which the will rebels against reason and becomes a slave at the command of passions. Just as the good can be loved for its own sake, as something intrinsically desired, so evil can be willed for its own sake. That's when someone's moral sense becomes desensitized, making evil appear to be good, or at least enjoyable. It creates another stain on one's soul. Stains like these need to be cured by what is called *confession*.

Thanks to confession, no disruption of our relationship with God needs to be forever. Healing through confession is a sign of God's immense mercy and forgiveness. For Catholics, there is no "forever," as long as there is the Sacrament of Confession. It brings reconciliation with God. It may look like an "easy way out," but the Catholic practice of frequent confession is certainly not meant to encourage sin, for it requires quite some humility to confess one's sins over and over again as a form of repentance. Instead, frequent confession is a perpetual acknowledgement of our brokenness.

Many people underestimate the power of confession. Scientists and health care providers may have tried to convince us that sinfulness is just a matter of sickness, genes, and chemicals—thus finding ways to get rid of its moral and religious dimension. But there is much reason to question this explanation. Maybe addictions can be healed better by religious conversion than by medication. Perhaps child abuse can be cured better with self-discipline than with sedatives. Possibly sexual abuse of children is not based on a pedophilia gene but on utterly sinful behavior—another form of rape that requires self-discipline rather than genetic manipulation. It could very well be that a guilt complex—another name for a syndrome—doesn't require a shrink session but rather the therapy of the confessional.

When asked “Why did you join the Church of Rome?” G.K. Chesterton answered in his autobiography as follows: “‘To get rid of my sins.’ For there is no other religious system that does really profess to get rid of people’s sins.” How right Chesterton was—the Catholic Church is unquestionably a “hospital for sinners,” perhaps even a “field hospital.” There is no better place to get rid of our sins.

One more question might still be lingering: Doesn’t the frequency of Confession in Catholicism make all of this a revolving-door event? It depends on how you look at it. Our sins keep piling up every day we live. Thanks to confession, Catholics don’t have to carry and heap up this increasing load of sins, for they can at any time unload their sins, and start with a “clean slate”—which does not mean, of course, the “slate” will stay clean. The practice of Confession acknowledges that God is a God of Justice who requires our repentance, but also a God of Mercy who is willing to accept our repentance over and over again—as long as we are willing to ask.

6. The Glory of Suffering

The Man Job

What are we to do with all the suffering in this broken world, inhabited by broken souls, broken hearts, broken families, and broken generations? There are some therapies, remedies, and cures that may soften the brokenness, but they can never really take our brokenness away. Brokenness seems to be an intrinsic part of human life on earth since the Fall in Paradise. Other than broken bones, there is no brokenness in the animal world—no broken souls, no broken hearts, no broke families, no broken generations. There was no such brokenness in the world until humanity appeared. But since the Fall, brokenness has become part of the human condition.

Probably the most down-to-earth account of human brokenness in the Bible can be found in the Book of Job. Here is what the account tells us. A good and happy family is stricken by one disaster after another, with no end in sight. A magnificent man, Job, loses everything and is left to sit on the ruins of his life. Forever, Job will be the unforgettable image of the just man unjustly afflicted. He is the central figure of a story that has intrigued generation after generation. We watch how all hell breaks loose in Job's life. What is reported to him sounds like a devastating litany: Robbers came, took your cattle and killed your servants...; a thunderstorm came, the sheep and servants were consumed by lightening...; enemies attacked us, raided your camels and killed your servants...; a big storm arose and struck the house of your oldest son, all your children were killed.... All in all, it's a litany of bad tidings, at least four in a row. The end result is this: Job is completely ruined.

It is a story similar to what many people have experienced themselves when all they had was destroyed by wild fires, hurricanes, tornadoes, or floods. Job 1:13-20 tells the disasters more extensively and detailed:

> *One day when Job's sons and daughters were feasting and drinking wine at the oldest brother's house, a messenger came to Job and said, "The oxen were plowing and the donkeys were grazing nearby, and the Sabeans attacked and carried them off. They put the servants to the sword, and I am the only one who has escaped to tell you!"*
>
> *While he was still speaking, another messenger came and said, "The fire of God fell from the sky and burned up the sheep and the servants, and I am the only one who has escaped to tell you!"*
>
> *While he was still speaking, another messenger came and said, "The Chaldeans formed three raiding parties and swept down on your camels and carried them off. They put the servants to the sword, and I am the only one who has escaped to tell you!"*
>
> *While he was still speaking, yet another messenger came and said, "Your sons and daughters were feasting and drinking wine at the oldest brother's house, when suddenly a mighty wind swept in from the desert and struck the four corners of the house. It collapsed on*

> *them and they are dead, and I am the only one who has escaped to tell you!"*

The devastation could not have been more complete. And yet, Job's reaction is royal. He does not get bitter but better. He stands up, tears his robe, shaves his head, falls upon the ground in worship, saying: "Naked I came from my mother's womb, and naked I will depart." He even utters: "The Lord gave and the Lord has taken away; may the name of the Lord be praised" (Job 1:21). In fact, Job has nothing left but his bare and naked faith, which makes him utter: I don't understand it, I cannot make sense of it, I don't know what to do with it—and yet, I refuse to curse God.

But the troubles are not over yet for Job. All that had happened so far was the loss of material things, not his health, neither physical nor spiritual. But now Job himself gets hit. The result is a sick and pitiful little creature, smitten from head to toe with painful sores which caused his skin to turn black and gave him a fever. Look at Job, completely covered with sores. People watch him with horror and disgust, as do his friends. There is nothing beautiful or noble about his misery. He is just plain dirt, unpleasant to look at, broken to the core. Not only has he lost everything he had, but now he is a wreck of a human being himself. This man is ruined for life.

We see Job sitting on the ruins of his life; he has been plunged into deep misery. How more broken can one be! Now watch his wife approach. Isn't she true to life in the way she reacts: Where did all your faithfulness get you? Damn God and die! We understand her only too well. Wasn't Job's misery also hers? Weren't his children also hers? And what about this pitiful human being himself—her husband of all people! Yet, Job's response is magnificent again, "You speak as foolish women do. We accept good things from God; should we not accept evil?" He is somehow saying: I always accepted the good things as being God-sent; He is so good to me, that I'm willing to receive from His hand the bad as well.

The book could have ended after these edifying words. It would have made for an edifying story, a reviver for believers. However, the story continues, because it's time now for the real tribulations. They don't come from Job's enemies but from his friends. Job's comforters! Isn't it true that prosperity makes friends, and adversity tries them? Job's friends are the ones who have all the answers to the horrible riddles of his misery. But their words turn out to be more painful than the sores on his body. Job still has depths to cross, deeper than his inexplicable and unreasonable misery.

Job's comforters resemble some people we know ourselves too well: they are the ones who give a quasi-religious twist to human suffering. One of them basically tells Job that one gets what one deserves and that one deserves what one gets. A second one explains that suffering is God's punishment for what we ourselves did wrong. A third one stresses that God's wisdom through suffering is entirely beyond human understanding because God's justice is not like ours. Another one strikes a different tone and explains suffering as a divine form of education, bringing people back to their senses. All nice trials, but do they satisfy Job?

After hearing all their semi-pious words and semi-religious explanations for his suffering, Job can no longer hold back:

> *Perish the day on which I was born, the night when they said, "The child is a boy!" May that day be darkness.... Why did I not die at birth, come forth from the womb and expire? Why did*

> *knees receive me, or breasts nurse me?... Or why was I not buried away like a stillborn child, like babies that have never seen the light?... Why is light given to the toilers, life to the bitter in spirit? They wait for death and it does not come; they search for it more than for hidden treasures.... For to me sighing comes more readily than food; my groans well forth like water. For what I feared overtakes me; what I dreaded comes upon me. I have no peace nor ease; I have no rest, for trouble has come!*

These are harsh words, especially when coming out of the mouth of a devout believer. But let's not be too quick to judge Job. To begin with, notice that it is not God whom he curses, but the day of his birth and the fact that he is alive. He doesn't say: Oh God, there is no God! What he does say is this: I wish I had not been born! He doesn't question: Is *God* really there for me? Actually, he is asking: Why am *I* here? Why did God create me? This tells us that Job hasn't removed God's address from his list; God remains the only address for him to come to with his why-questions. If there is any answer, any solution, or any explanation available, then they are to be found with God. In fact, arguing with God makes for a more religious attitude towards life than having a philosophy that doesn't acknowledge God as one's Creator. The person arguing with God is not considered as someone who has lost faith, but as someone who does the ultimate to hold on to God, even in times of disaster.

Nevertheless, for Job, there is still this tremendous question, the most nagging question there is: "Why is light given to those in misery, and life to the bitter of soul?" (Job 3:20). Why was I given life if it holds so much misery? I don't remember asking for it, Job must have thought. What is the purpose of this misery? And why is this broken world in existence, why all of our history, why this long martyrdom of countless broken generations of people? Why did all of this have to happen—a broken world with broken generations, broken families, broken hearts, broken souls?

Job actually rejected all the "blasphemous answers" that his so-called friends gave him about God. Job keeps repeating that a God who hits back is not the God he knows. And the entire Bible stands behind him: Evil and suffering *do* exist but *shouldn't* exist; they may be part of *life* but not of *creation*. Job's "comforters," who have all the answers to his piercing questions, turn out to be in fact his "adversaries," who provide cover-ups for all the suffering in the world—thereby changing God into an enemy. The Apostle James makes a very strong case: "Let no one say when he is tempted, 'I am tempted by God'; for God cannot be tempted with evil and he himself tempts no one" (Jas. 1:13). It is the devil who tempts. That's why the Book of Job starts with introducing the devil.

Job, for his part, keeps repeating to his friends that he did not lose his faith in God. No, Job hasn't lost God at all when he exclaims those eternal words well known from Handel's *Messiah*: "I know that my Redeemer liveth" (19:25)—which means "I know..." that God is God-*with*-us (*Emmanuel*), not God-*against*-us. To many people, Handel's Messiah has one of the most touching pieces of music ever composed. It is an Easter song. Not too many people realize, though, that this beaming profession of faith has been snatched from between the harsh lamentations and bitter accusations uttered by the afflicted Job, suffering under his pain and grief, and suffering from the semi-pious words his friends had voiced as explanations for his troubles.

The text speaks of a *redeemer*, a familiar concept in the Old

Testament. Even if you have gone aground, even if you have to sell your land, even if you have to sell yourself as a servant, never will you get lost forever. The Law of Moses commands your closest relatives to buy your land, or to ransom you as a person, someday. A redeemer, or vindicator, is someone who releases you from your desperate circumstances. If you happen to die without having children—that is to say, in Jewish terms, without having a future—the redeemer has the duty to marry your widow, thus ensuring you a future.

In spite of all his setbacks, materially and spiritually, Job remains firm in his stand, in his belief in a redeemer. He tells his friends that the God he knows would never do what they are telling him. Evil and suffering are too serious and too devastating to blame God for them. Therefore, Job keeps asking for *God*'s personal answer instead. Well, did Job really get an answer from God?

Yes, Job did receive an answer from God—perhaps not on first sight. At the end of the book, God seems to bombard Job's questions with a cascade of counter-questions: Where were you, Job, when I did this? Where were you when I did that? It is turning Job's repeated question of "Where were you, God, when I was stricken by misery?" into a counter-question of "Where were you, Job, when...?" In fact, it is not an answer but one long-winded question, consisting of a collection of sentences, all of them devastating questions, until the very end.

However, do not read God's torrent of questions the wrong way. It is not anticipating an answer like "you were nowhere and you are nothing." God's answer is not meant in a demeaning way. We would seriously be mistaken to stick to our first impression, to consider this to be a sarcastic way of putting Job down by giving him a description of the majesty and loftiness of the Creator and His creation compared to the tininess of Job. Something else is at stake here. A few sentences may put us on the right track: "Who shut up the sea behind doors, when it burst forth from the womb?" (Job 38:8). "Have you ever given orders to the morning, or shown the dawn its place?" (Job 38:12). "Have you an arm like that of God?" (Job 40:9). In other words, God is asking Job: Don't you remember how I shut up the sea, a menace to life, how I created light in the darkness to light up your path, and how I use my arm to protect people like you? Have you forgotten all of that, Job? Have you forgotten, Job, that God's creation was *good*, from day one on.

To come straight to the point: God is expressing his intense concern over his creation, especially over his people. It's for them and for their sake that everything exists. In fact, it's a colossal home furnished with tender loving care. In other words, it is *I*, a caring God, who created all of this—a home furnished with TLC. God is asking: You, human being, have you ever looked at it this way? Have you ever read my heart this way? Such is the very question God is asking Job, out of mere concern; there is no sarcasm involved at all.

So God's answer to Job was not really an answer the way we understand it. Besides, if Job was told that God's creation was done with TLC, there is still the question left where evil comes from in what God has created. The Book of Job comes up only with the beginning of an answer. It mentions the role of Satan at the beginning and the end of the book. In other words, evil is not something God created, but his enemy does. It's just a dawning insight, perhaps not even a clear answer yet.

Let me put it differently: Did Job actually expect an answer? To have all riddles solved and all questions answered, is that really what Job was waiting for? Job does not need a kind of God who gives us all the answers. What he needs is a God who is *answering* him. He needs God Himself. He needs to know where he stands with God; he needs to know whether God is with him, or against him. And it's that very need that God met. Job understands. He understands what he hears: Job, I am on your side; you should know that!

God's answer to Job may not look like an answer in the technical sense—it is not even God's final answer. That final answer came much later. God's ultimate answer would come in the form of a person, directly from Heaven: the God-Man Jesus. In Jesus, we find the ultimate answer and cure for our broken hearts and our broken world. This "answer" does not come from words but from a person, the Son of God. It is an answer that comes in fact from the Man of Golgotha: God is love—and love wants to share to the very end, with all its consequences. God's love wants to personally share everything with us, even our sufferings.

So Jesus came, not to abolish, but to sanctify suffering with his presence. Jesus did not save us *from* the cross, but instead he saved us *by* the Cross. Anyone who offers love without sacrifice, anyone who offers Christ without the Cross, is just trying to sell snake oil. Even in suffering—or particularly in suffering—we can find the Glory of God, for Jesus is the human face of God—and a human face comes with tears. Our tears are his tears, for God is not a God of evil but a God of love. Through the Incarnation, God entered space and time, which comes with suffering. Pope Benedict XVI summarized this well during his *Urbi et Orbi* blessing on Christmas Day 2011 with one single sentence: "Jesus Christ is the proof that God has heard our cry." Indeed, he is a compassionate God. Seen from this angle, even suffering can become a blessing. Put differently, there can be glory in suffering.

The Man Abraham

Let's state first that the Judeo-Christian faith is in essence the only world religion that takes suffering seriously. Other religions may gloss over the issue but do not really know what to do with it. Christianity, on the other hand, is even more emphatic about suffering than Judaism, because it believes that the only therapy—if you want to call it that way—for all brokenness in the world is to be found in the Cross of Golgotha. That makes Christianity really unique, even within the context of the Judeo-Christian tradition. Although Pope Pius XI said about Christians, "Spiritually we are Semites," even the Jews of the Old Testament were not quite able to deal with suffering (yet).

For many centuries, the Jews of the Old Testament thought that prosperity and happiness are signs that God is on our side, whereas poverty and suffering tell us God is not. Even in the Book of Job, this old idea did creep in at the end of the book: "The Lord also restored the prosperity of Job, after he had prayed for his friends; the Lord even gave to Job twice as much as he had before.... Thus the Lord blessed the later days of Job more than his earlier ones. Now he had fourteen thousand sheep, six thousand camels, a thousand yoke of oxen, and a thousand she-donkeys" (Job 42:10,12). This almost makes for a rather cheap ending.

Gradually, though, the truth about suffering began to dawn in early Judaism. The prophet Jeremiah dared to ask, "Why does the way of the wicked prosper? Why do all the faithless live at ease?" (Jer. 12:1). Isn't that contrary to the belief that the closer to God we are, the less we suffer, and that evil suffered is evil deserved? And the Book of Ecclesiastes (Kohelet in Hebrew) minces no words when it states, "I have seen both of these: a righteous man perishing in his righteousness, and a wicked man living long in his wickedness" (Eccl. 7:15). But in spite of these dawning insights, suffering remained a stumbling block in Judaism.

Gradually, though, there were some more rays of light appearing in the Jewish struggle with suffering. The Prophet Isaiah describes a mysterious figure who bore our sufferings and endured our infirmities: "He was pierced for our offenses, crushed for our sin; upon him was the chastisement that makes us whole, by his stripes we were healed" (Is. 53:5). The more technical term for this kind of suffering is *vicarious* suffering—the suffering of one person that can substitute or relieve the suffering of others.

The idea of one-for-many has a much longer history in the Old Testament—this time not the suffering of one-for-many but the righteousness of one-for-many. This latter belief features strongly in the famous story about Abraham's plea for Sodom. When asking God, "Will you indeed destroy the righteous with the wicked?", Abraham starts negotiating: Suppose there are fifty righteous within the city, will you then destroy the place and not spare it for the fifty righteous who are in it? Next, Abraham whittles this plea farther down: What about forty-five? What about forty? What about thirty? Suppose twenty are found there? At last, he gets God down to ten: "For the sake of ten I will not destroy it." The Man Abraham appealed to God on the basis of ten-to-many—and so would his descendants.

This story of Abraham has a sequel, counting farther down from ten-to-one, when God says to the prophet Jeremiah about Jerusalem: "Run back and forth through the streets of Jerusalem.... Search her squares to see if you can find a man, one who does justice and seeks the truth; that I may pardon her." Ultimately, that one man will be found in Jesus of Nazareth, the Son of Man, the Christ, the God-Man, our Savior and Redeemer. It was the High Priest Caiaphas who spoke to the Sanhedrin these prophetic words: "One man should die for the people" (John 11:50). That's where vicarious suffering comes in—the suffering of one-for-many.

There is something very peculiar going on here. We tend to ask God here not to treat the just the way the unjust deserve to be treated, but, instead, God decides to treat the unjust in the same way he treats the just, as if they were just, too. God, in fact, somehow pardons the unjust majority because of the tiny just minority. This was also the "mission" of Jesus Christ—through him, and him alone, humanity would be pardoned and redeemed from Sin. Jesus gave us our human dignity back, but at the cost of his own. Each time we ask God "Why me?", we should listen carefully to hear Jesus whisper in response, "Why me?"

At this point the vicarious *righteousness* of one-for-many has turned into the vicarious *suffering* of one-for-many. Jesus is the one suffering for many. It is very tempting to connect Jesus' story in the New Testament with Abraham's story in the Old Testament, when God said to Abraham, "Take your son Isaac, your only one, whom you love, and go to the land of Moriah. Offer him up there as a burnt offering on one of the heights that I will point out to you" (Gen. 22:2). There is the Man Abraham again. And then the story continues:

> *Early the next morning Abraham saddled his donkey, took with him two of his servants and his son Isaac, and after cutting the wood for the burnt offering, set out for the place of which God had told him. On the third day Abraham caught sight of the place from a distance. Abraham said*

> *to his servants: "Stay here with the donkey, while the boy and I go on over there. We will worship and then come back to you." So Abraham took the wood for the burnt offering and laid it on his son Isaac, while he himself carried the fire and the knife. As the two walked on together, Isaac spoke to his father Abraham. "Father!" he said. "Here I am," he replied. Isaac continued, "Here are the fire and the wood, but where is the sheep for the burnt offering?" "My son," Abraham answered, "God will provide the sheep for the burnt offering." Then the two walked on together.*
>
> *When they came to the place of which God had told him, Abraham built an altar there and arranged the wood on it. Next he bound his son Isaac, and put him on top of the wood on the altar. Then Abraham reached out and took the knife to slaughter his son. But the angel of the Lord called to him from heaven, "Abraham, Abraham!" "Here I am," he answered. "Do not lay your hand on the boy," said the angel. "Do not do the least thing to him. For now I know that you fear God, since you did not withhold from me your son, your only one."*

A rather recent similarity to Isaac's journey can be found in Poland during World War II. On August 5, 1942, the Nazis came to round up the 192 Jewish orphans in Korczak's care to take them to Treblinka. For reasons that remain unknown, Korczak himself was offered amnesty by the Nazis and passage to the Polish side of the Jewish Ghetto walls. He refused, insisting he wanted to go with the children to suffer with them on their way to the "altar." Eyewitness Joshua Perle described the scene:

> *A miracle occurred. Two hundred children did not cry. Two hundred pure souls, condemned to*

> *death, did not weep. Not one of them ran away. None tried to hide. Like stricken swallows they clung to their teacher and mentor, to their father and brother, Janusz Korczak, so that he might protect and preserve them.... A few nurses were followed by two hundred children, dressed in clean and meticulously cared for clothes, as they were being carried to the altar.*

Korczak's evacuation from the Ghetto is also mentioned in Władysław Szpilman's book *The Pianist*:

> *He told the orphans they were going out into the country, so they ought to be cheerful. At last they would be able to exchange the horrible suffocating city walls for meadows of flowers, streams where they could bathe, woods full of berries and mushrooms. He told them to wear their best clothes, and so they came out into the yard, two by two, nicely dressed and in a happy mood. The little column was led by an SS man.*

The God-Man Jesus

The story of Abraham and his son Isaac has been considered by Christians as a profound allegory for the sacrifice of the God-Man Jesus on the Cross. Just like Isaac was Abraham's beloved son, so was Jesus the Father's only beloved son. Like Isaac, Jesus carried uphill the wood for his own sacrifice. When Isaac asks, "where is the sheep for the burnt offering?" Abraham answered in a way that proved to be prophetic. How so? Since there is no punctuation in the Hebrew original, verse 8 of Genesis 22 could be read as follows: "God will provide himself, the Lamb, for a burnt offering"—the Lamb being Jesus Christ, God himself.

Like Job and Abraham and countless others, Jesus learned

what it means to live in a broken world. He was betrayed by Judas. He was abandoned by his other followers. He was taken captive by a mob. He was deserted by his disciples. He was falsely accused and rejected by Jewish leaders. He was mocked and abused by Roman guards. He was spat upon and beaten up. He was falsely accused by those in authority. He was rejected by the crowd. He was scourged. He was spit upon and struck on the head. And finally he was crucified between two thieves—the cruelest method of execution we know of in human history. If there is one thing we can thank Mel Gibson for, it is his showing us the graphic and torturous nature of the crucifixion in his movie, *The Passion of the Christ*.

But unlike Job and Abraham, Jesus was not merely a Man but he was the *God*-Man. He was not a Man like Job or Abraham, but a God-Man. That's the crucial difference between Jesus of Nazareth and other human beings in history. The Christian belief that Jesus was not only the Messiah but also the Son of God can be found all over the New Testament. Immediately after Paul's conversion, "he began at once to proclaim Jesus in the synagogues, that he is the *Son of God*" (Acts 9: 20). This belief is also very prevalent in the most recent Gospel, John's; but even in the oldest Gospel, Mark's, we find this belief repeatedly proclaimed—for instance, at his baptism by John the Baptizer, "And a voice came from the heavens, 'You are my beloved Son; with you I am well pleased'" (Mk. 1:11). And during the Transfiguration, "then from the cloud came a voice, 'This is my beloved Son. Listen to him'" (Mk. 9:7). When the high priest asked him, "Are you the Christ, the Son of God?" (Mk. 11:33), Jesus replied yes and was immediately sentenced to death. John's Gospel (5:18) makes it also very clear that Jesus was condemned by the Jews because of his proclaimed equality with God: "For this reason the Jews tried all the more to kill him, because he not only broke the Sabbath but he also called God his own father, making himself equal to God."

It is at the heart of Catholic faith, not merely that God exists, but that he took on human flesh at the moment of the Incarnation. In other words, Jesus is God who became Man—God-made-flesh. This means Jesus is in fact *God* (but you cannot reverse it, for God is more than Jesus). When the Son of God came into the flesh—which is the Incarnation—he renounced his dignity, as it were, but not his divinity. One of the earliest Church Fathers, St. Justin (100-165), put it very emphatically: "The Church confesses that Jesus is the Son of God who came in flesh. This is the scandal and this is why they persecuted Jesus."

At St. Paul's time, preaching the Crucifixion was a scandal—a scandal for Roman, Greek, and Jewish ears—but although not mentioned explicitly, the Incarnation was a scandal, too. Especially for modern ears, preaching the Incarnation is as scandalous as preaching the Crucifixion. How could it possibly be that God became man? How could it possibly be that the Word became flesh? If there is any belief in God left nowadays, it is mostly a belief in a lofty, transcendent God, who is infinitely far above and beyond us human beings. What the Incarnation idea portrays, according to this view, is at best a regression to paganism, to the Greek and Roman pantheon, where gods act like human beings.

But not so in Christianity. The Incarnation is the mystery of the God-Man. That means God is the son of a human mother, and a human woman is the mother of God. Isn't that hard to believe? And yet, it's the greatest story ever told: the one, true God taking on human flesh. The light of the world entered the darkness of a woman's womb. The God-Man Jesus came to be among sinners and came to die so that we, the sinners, might live. As the 5th-century philosopher Proclus put it, "We do not proclaim a deified man, but we confess an incarnate God."

It is to be expected that the mystery of the Incarnation has been misunderstood in many ways. There are at least two extreme misconceptions—either Jesus was only man or Jesus was only God.

One misconception about Jesus—technically it's called a heresy—is the idea that Jesus was God but not a man. If Jesus is indeed the Son of God, then he cannot be completely human at the same time, so it's said. How could the Creator of the Universe ever become a baby in a manger? How could we possibly accept the sentence, "the Word was made flesh," in a literal sense? God is in his remote Heaven, far away from filthy flesh. This view makes the idea of the Incarnation as much a scandal as the idea of the Crucifixion! Both cannot be real! When the apostles thought they had walked and talked with Jesus, they must have actually walked and talked with a mirage, a ghost from heaven. This mirage could not possibly be born nor have suffered real pain, certainly not on the Cross. In other words, Jesus had only taken on the *appearance* of a man—a "make-believe" person. His life on earth and his suffering on the Cross were nothing but a divine stunt of playacting. Jesus' body just looked like flesh but wasn't flesh. Christ only *seemed* to possess a body, to suffer, and to die. If Jesus had no real flesh, then his crucifixion must also have been "make-believe."

The other misconception about Jesus is the opposite idea: that Jesus was a man but not God. This leads to many questions. How could a God-man ever suffer? How could

Jesus be God, for there is only one God—not two or three of them? If God is one, then how could Jesus be God as well. This idea made some say that Jesus himself was not God but was merely adopted by God. The adopted son was able to suffer, but not so the Son of God. Although he is called "the Son of God," he is only an adoptive son. He was truly man, but not truly God.

Both views are misconceptions because they break the mysterious tension of "God is one, yet God is three" and "Jesus is human, yet Jesus is divine." They do so by making a choice and thus eliminating one of the two sides of the seeming paradox. Breaking this tension actually makes the Good News collapse. Why?

Why is the fact that Jesus is the God-Man—not only man but also God—so vital for the healing of our broken existence? The first Christians and the early Church Fathers saw very clearly that the deity of Christ is in fact the cornerstone of our salvation. Jesus could have only redeemed us if he was God and yet really and truly gave his body for our bodies, and his flesh for our flesh—otherwise our redemption would be null and void, and he would have suffered for nothing. A broken world can only be healed by the one who created this world, God. In a recent interview, Pope Benedict XVI made the same point. After mentioning all the evils we have witnessed now and in the past, he continues,

> *This mass of evil cannot simply be declared nonexistent, not even by God. It must be cleansed, reworked and overcome.... God simply cannot leave "as is" the mass of evil that comes from the freedom that He Himself has granted. Only He, coming to share in the world's suffering, can redeem the world.... When the Son struggles in the Garden of Olives with the will of*

> *the Father, it is not a matter of accepting for himself a cruel disposition of God, but rather of attracting humanity into the very will of God.*

If Christ were only a creature, however, the Gospel would not truly be such good news after all. Therefore, it's vital to Christianity that Jesus was truly God and truly man, both Son of God and Son of Man—in short, the God-Man. If Jesus is not God but merely a human being, then his words and actions are worth as much, or rather as little, as anyone else's—which is not much.

In other words, the power of Jesus' Crucifixion was only possible through the mystery of his Incarnation—the *Word* made flesh, the coming of *God* into the flesh. The late Supreme Court Judge Antonin Scalia told us once the story of the best lesson he ever learned during his studies at Georgetown University. It happened during his oral comprehensive examination at the end of his senior year. His history professor, Dr. Wilkinson, asked him one last question: "Of all the historical events you have studied, which one in your opinion had the most impact upon the world?" Scalia mulled over several options: the French Revolution, the Battle of Lepanto, or perhaps the American Revolution? Whatever he eventually chose to answer, Dr. Wilkinson informed him of the right answer. Of course, it was the Incarnation, which ultimately led to the Crucifixion and the Resurrection. A real turning point in history!

Without Jesus' Crucifixion, there would not have been a Resurrection. This is best epitomized in what the Bible (John 20:24-29) tells us about the Apostle Thomas, also called Didymus, but probable better known as "doubting Thomas." When Jesus had appeared to his disciples, after he was crucified and buried, Thomas was not with them when Jesus came. So, when the other disciples said to him, "We have seen the Lord," Thomas said to them, "Unless I see the mark of the nails in his hands and put my finger into the nail marks and put my hand into his side, I will not believe." Thomas could not have expressed better that he didn't believe in a Resurrection without a Crucifixion. The scars of the Crucifixion are the best guarantee of the truth of the Resurrection.

On the other hand, without Jesus' Incarnation, his Crucifixion would have been meaningless. Through the Incarnation, the God-Man entered space and time, which includes our suffering—and through his suffering our salvation. With the coming of God's Son, who alone can remove Original Sin, it will be possible for a redeemed humanity to live eventually in an ideal world free from suffering—which is the Kingdom of Heaven, a broken world restored. It all revolves around Original Sin, the endemic state of a broken world. The God-Man Jesus went to the full depth of sin and suffering on Golgotha by identifying himself with our suffering in order to eradicate the effects of sin. This is the mystery of the Incarnation, and thus of the Crucifixion—the fact that that the God-Man Jesus comes to us, weeps with us, and suffers with us.

But don't take this the wrong way. This does not mean that God is a suffering God. A god who suffers is not God. If suffering would affect God as much as it affects us, there would be little hope left for all of us who are suffering. The idea of a "suffering God" is based on the erroneous idea that there is only one Person in the Godhead, so that the Father, the Son, and the Holy Spirit are all one person—rather than three Persons. Simply put again, Jesus is God—but this doesn't mean God is Jesus. God is "Father, Son, and Holy Spirit." The Father is not the Son, and the Son is not the Father; they are both "one" by not being each other. When the Son of God suffered, it was not God the Father who experienced the sufferings. With Jesus' suffering, the God-the-Son was in pain, but God-the-Father remained in charge, as is shown in the Resurrection. Had Jesus only suffered as a *divine* being, then his teaching would have been useless for *human* beings. With Jesus' suffering, the God-the-Son was in pain, but God-the-Father was in charge. As Pope St. Leo the Great said about Jesus's suffering, "Being God who cannot suffer, he did not disdain to be man that can suffer."

There is another important reason why God cannot suffer. If the suffering of creatures would really cause the Creator himself to suffer, this idea would place both on the same level. As a consequence, there would be no hope for us of ever being freed from suffering. What human beings cry out for in their suffering is not a god who suffers, but a God who loves wholly and completely. A god-in-pain, on the other hand, is no longer God, let alone a God-in-charge. If God were as vulnerable as we are, we would be in real trouble. For our redemption, we need a God-in-charge, not a God-in-pain. Because God the Father is in charge, God will not be devastated by suffering. The Good News of the Crucifixion is that we are not suffering alone—God is suffering-with-us in his Son Jesus on the Cross. But it is crucial to keep in mind that when the Lord Jesus suffered it was his humanity that suffered—not his divinity.

The God-Man Jesus on earth prays as man, he obeys as man, and he suffers as man. The form of God had departed from him, for by emptying himself of it, he had taken the form of a servant. So his *divine* nature had not ceased to be but had taken upon itself the humility of *human* birth. As St. Paul said, "Rather, he emptied himself, taking the form of a slave, coming in human likeness; and found human in appearance, he humbled himself, becoming obedient to death, even death on a cross" (Eph. 2:7-8).

No wonder, then, that there is power in the Cross. In Dan Schutte's *Easter Triduum Hymn*, every stance ends with the words, "Let us ever glory in the Cross of Christ." You might wonder how there could ever be *glory* in the Cross. How could the Cross ever triumph over human brokenness? That's something hard to believe, until we realize that we do have reason to speak of the "Glory of the Cross" because it was not the cross of a man called Jesus, but the Cross of the *God*-Man Jesus. At the Cross, the God-Man Jesus took on the brokenness of the entire world, of all generations, of all families, of all hearts, and of all souls.

Golgotha is all about the curse of brokenness we experience daily in soul, heart, family, generation, and the world. The message of Golgotha is that God is love—and love wants to share. God's love wants to share everything with us, even our sufferings. We can meet God everywhere, even on Golgotha of all places. When we ask Jesus how much he loves us, he will tell us "This much..." while spreading his arms and dying for us. No wonder, the Gospel of John tells us, "God sent the Son into the world, not to condemn the world, but that the world might be saved through him." Jesus came, not to abolish, but to sanctify suffering with his presence. Jesus did not save us *from* the cross, but instead he saved us *by* the cross. Even in suffering—or particularly in suffering—we can find the Glory of God, for Jesus is the human face of God—and a human face comes with tears. As the late Fr. Benedict Groeschel put it, "This is the mystery of the Incarnation. Christ comes and weeps with us. He suffers with us." Seen from this angle, even suffering can at times become a blessing.

But our questions remain. Is there hope for a broken world,

with its broken generations, families, hearts, and souls? The answer is: Yes, there is hope because the God-Man Jesus remains patient with us and was willing to die for us, without mumbling a word. There is a Negro Spiritual that puts it so well:

> *1 They crucified my Lord, / and he never said a mumbalin' word; / they crucified my Lord, / and he never said a mumbalin' word. / Not a word, not a word, not a word. / 2 They nailed him to a tree, / and he never said a mumbalin' word; / they nailed him to a tree, / and he never said a mumbalin' word. / Not a word, not a word, not a word.*

Years ago, in 1953, the late German Noble Laureate Heinrich Böll wrote a novel with the title *Und sagte kein einziges Wort* ("And Never Said a Word"). It is a simple, but disturbing, daily-life story of two married people. The man becomes an alcoholic, leaves his family, and cannot handle life anymore. But he is helped in his brokenness by returning back to them and by the unwavering love of his wife who suffers with him without saying a word. She silently helps him with a love that never gives up. It is a hidden reference—Böll was Catholic—to the story of Jesus who did not say a word either when he was on his way to the cross out of love for all of us.

Then there is this play called *The Plague in Bergamo* by Jens Peter Jacobsen (1847-1885) which tells us about the power of Jesus' Cross in a very dramatic way. It is about a town in Italy during the Middle Ages when the plague had broken out. It portrays how, at the very beginning when the plague broke out, people worked together in harmony and concord. They took care that the corpses were duly and properly buried. But above all else, the people went to the churches early and late, alone and in processions. Every day they went with their prayers before God. But all this did not help; there was nothing that helped.

When they began to believe that heaven either would not or could not help, they gave up. It seemed as if sin had grown from a secret, stealthy disease into a wicked, open, raging plague, which—hand in hand with the physical contagion—sought to slay the soul as the other strove to destroy the body. The air was filled with blasphemy and impiety. The mob was even desecrating the church.

But then a group of strangers from a neighboring village entered the church, led by a young monk. He raised his thin, sickly hands toward heaven in prayer, and the sleeves of his robe slipped down over his lean, white arms. Then he spoke:

> *You build upon the cross of Golgotha, come, come! Come and look at it! I shall lead you straight to its foot.... And He on the cross looked down on the soldiers, who were casting lots for His unstitched garment and down on the whole turbulent mob, for whose sake He suffered, that they might be saved; and in all the multitude there was not one pitiful eye.*
>
> *And those below looked up toward Him, who hung there suffering and weak; they looked at the tablet above His head, whereon was written "King of the Jews," and they reviled Him and called out to Him: "Thou that destroyest the temple, and buildest it in three days, save thyself. If thou be the Son of God, come down from the cross." Then He, the only begotten Son of God was taken with anger, and saw that they were not worthy of salvation, these mobs that fill the earth.... Then He leaped down upon the earth.... And the cross stood empty, and the great work of*

> *redemption was never fulfilled. There is no mediator between God and us; there is no Jesus who died for us on the cross; there is no Jesus who died for us on the cross, there is no Jesus who died for us on the cross!*

When the monk fell silent, one of the people in the crowd pushed forward with raised, threatening hands, pale as a corpse, and shouted: "Monk, monk, you must nail Him on the cross again, you must!" And behind him there was a hoarse, hissing sound: "Yea, yea, crucify, crucify Him!" And from all mouths rose a storm of cries up to the vaulted roof: "Crucify, crucify Him!"

This may sound like a depressing, blasphemous story, but it brings one point across in a very powerful way: without Jesus' Cross we are indeed all lost. Had he come down from the cross, we would all still not be saved from our brokenness. Whenever we ask God "Why me?", to stress the point again, we may actually hear Jesus whisper in response "Why Me?" And we know the answer. The doctrine of the Original Sin can only be understood in the light of the salvation Jesus "bought" for us. If there is no Original Sin, then the Cross is a hoax; if the Cross is a hoax, then the whole economy of salvation is up for grabs. In the words of the Catechism (389):

> *The doctrine of original sin is, so to speak, the "reverse side" of the Good News that Jesus is the Savior of all men, that all need salvation and that salvation is offered to all through Christ. The Church, which has the mind of Christ, knows very well that we cannot tamper with the revelation of original sin without undermining the mystery of Christ.*

So, it shouldn't surprise us that the Crucifix became so

prominent in the Church. Whereas, in early Christian art, the Crucifixion was represented by the bare Latin cross, by the fifth century the body of Christ was painted on the cross, and later became a sculpture attached by four nails, one in each hand and foot. One of the earliest known representations of Christ being crucified is a fifth century panel on the brass door of Santa Sabina in Rome. The Church added the figure of Christ to remind the faithful of the great suffering that had brought about their redemption. Jesus had to suffer and *die* for us! He is the Lamb who takes away the sins of the world. No matter how strange it may sound, that's why we *glory* in the Cross. It was the most significant moment in human history. As St. Cyril of Jerusalem put it,

> *We proclaim the Crucified, and the devils quake. So don't be ashamed of the Cross of Christ. Openly seal it on your forehead that the devils may behold the royal sign and flee trembling far away. Make the sign of the Cross when you eat or drink, when you sit down, lie down, or get up. When you speak, when you walk—in a word, at every act.*

In the Book of Job we may not have received an answer to all Job's and our own questions about human suffering. But in the God-Man Jesus we did. Golgotha is the real answer to all our questions. The Apostle Peter reminds the early Christians of the true price of salvation. "You were ransomed from the futile ways inherited from your ancestors, not with perishable silver or gold, but with the precious blood of Christ." (1 Peter 1:18-19) And his fellow Apostle Paul concurs and draws the consequence: "You were bought with a price—so glorify God in your body!" (1 Cor. 6:20). That's why the Stations of the Cross have been so important in Catholicism. They show us at what price our redemption was "bought."

Glory in Our Own Crosses

After what we have seen so far, there is indeed glory in the Cross. But this is not only true about the Cross of the God-Man on Golgotha, but also about the personal, individual crosses that we all carry. Suffering is the "therapy" and "cure" to heal a broken world—not only the suffering of Jesus at the Cross of Golgotha, but also the suffering of each one of us going through suffering. The existence of suffering and adversity actually shows us that we are *not* in control of our lives but need assistance beyond human power. By the example of the God-Man Jesus, we may discover there is redemptive power in carrying our own crosses. St. Paul tells us we should never neglect the redemptive value of suffering: "Now I rejoice in what I am suffering for you" (Col. 1:24). It is only in a world where daily life has lost its *supernatural* dimension that suffering also loses its redemptive value.

Isn't it striking that Christianity actually has the Cross at center stage in its religion? It claims there is some mysterious salvation for us in carrying our crosses in life—that is, vicarious suffering for the benefit of ourselves and for the benefit of others. No wonder the Cross is a touchstone for Christians, but at the same time a stumbling block for non-believers. St. Paul was right when he called Christ crucified "a stumbling block to Jews and foolishness to Gentiles" (1 Cor. 1:23).

In other words, Golgotha has become a "meeting place" for all those who suffer. From now on, in the words of the Catechism (1521), "Suffering, a consequence of Original Sin, acquires a new meaning; it becomes a participation in the saving work of Jesus." In him, we are able to "offer up" our sufferings, for we are participants and co-workers in his creation. Not only Jesus' suffering but even our own sufferings can be for the salvation of others.

Needless to say that this is so much counter to our modern mindset. We live in a world that runs away from suffering; our bathroom cabinets are filled with painkillers. Since the time of our youth, we have been conditioned to view suffering as an impediment to happiness. This worldview, which is so deeply embedded in our culture, tells us that the less we suffer, the happier we will be. Yet, we could be missing out on another dimension of suffering, for suffering has this mysterious potential of redeeming us, transforming us, transfiguring us. You might think the less we suffer, the closer to God we will be—but it might actually be the opposite: the more we suffer, the closer to God we will be. Suffering provides those who suffer the ability to participate in their own and others' redemption from sin, through Jesus Christ. That's how suffering can become very therapeutic.

Many people agree that the loss of a child—even if they have not experienced such a loss themselves—is the heaviest cross a parent can bear and the worst suffering a parent can go through. This is not meant to belittle other crosses in a family life, but those who did go through the loss of a child will certainly know what I am trying to say. Michelle Fritz, for instance, is a homeschooling mother to eleven living children. She has experienced the loss of sixteen babies—yes, sixteen—so her testimony deserves to be heard. First of all, after much internal struggle, she could finally come to the awareness that "God knew my pain; He had lost His own Son too." Then she continues:

> *I thought about the pain, the suffering, the loneliness, the darkness, the healing, and the light. If someone had told me almost three years ago that I would be happy now I wouldn't have believed them. How could we go through hell and*

still be ok? When I was there, in the deepest, darkest parts of suffering, the light seemed so far away. The pain ripped at my heart every second of every day. It felt like it would never end. In a way I didn't want it to end. I felt it was all I had left to tie me to my precious babies. I was wrong. I had something so much more to remind me of the little ones I only held for such a short time. I had hope... the hope that one day I will hold them in Heaven once again.

In the beginning it was hard to pray. I was sad, angry, hurt, and felt alone. I didn't want to pray to a God that took my babies! Still, I knew that it was important to continue to pray. I also knew in my heart that God didn't take them as a punishment but it was easier to think of Him as the bad guy when I just didn't know what to think or believe. Thank goodness our Father is so understanding and loving... He took my accusations and shouldered them. He accepted my pain as His and held me even closer to Him. I began to pray the prayers I had memorized as a child. Thank goodness for those prayers as it was hard for me to pray in my own words at that time.

Christians often express their belief in the redemptive power of carrying their own crosses by saying to suffering people, "Offer up your suffering for someone else." Many people can testify to the power of vicarious suffering. Let me just mention a few examples; hopefully, you can recognize part of yourself in one or some of them.

The first example is St. Maximilian Kolbe. He was a Polish Franciscan priest, arrested by Nazis in February of 1941 for publishing unapproved literature. They sentenced him to hard labor at the concentration camp in Auschwitz. In

August of that year a prisoner escaped. When he was not recaptured, the Nazis took a reprisal. They lined up the other prisoners and picked out ten to die in the starvation bunker. One of the men selected was a farmer named Franciszek Gajowniczek. When Franciszek was selected, he cried out, "My wife, my children!" Hearing that cry, Fr. Kolbe stepped forward and said to the guard, "I am a Catholic priest. I have no family like this man. Allow me to take his place." The guard hesitated, then agreed.

Many years later, at the canonization ceremony of Fr. Kolbe in 1982, Pope John Paul II had a surprise which sent a thrill through the whole congregation. The man who had been sitting next to him during the homily was none other than Franciszek Gajowniczek. He survived the concentration camp and has devoted his life since to telling others what Fr. Kolbe did for him, taking his place, being a man-for-others like Jesus had been.

The second example is St. Edith Stein. Coming from a Jewish, atheistic background, she became a Catholic convert, when she visited a Christian friend who had recently lost her husband. When she saw the peace her friend had attained through acceptance of her cross, Edith met the Crucified Christ. At that moment, she tells us, Judaism paled and the Cross loomed high. Little did she know how thoroughly she would be trained in "the school of the Cross," as she called it. She became a Carmelite nun, but refused to go into hiding when Hitler took over in Germany. Eventually, she suffered a martyr's death in 1942 at Auschwitz. She had been convinced from the beginnings of National Socialism that it was the Cross of Christ being laid on the Jews, a continuation of his crucified humanity in time. She wanted a share in that.

Shortly before her death, Carmelite Sister Edith Stein said to a priest, "Who will do penance for the evil that the Germans are inflicting?" On the way to her crucifixion, the gas chamber at Auschwitz, she spoke of her suffering as an offering "for the conversion of atheists, for her fellow Jews, for the Nazi persecutors, and for all who no longer had the love of God in their hearts." She was another one who vicariously suffered for many.

In his homily during the canonization of Edith Stein, Pope John Paul II said:

> *Finally, the new saint teaches us that love for Christ undergoes suffering. Whoever truly loves does not stop at the prospect of suffering: he accepts communion in suffering with the one he loves. Aware of what her Jewish origins implied, Edith Stein spoke eloquently about them: "Beneath the Cross I understood the destiny of God's People.... Indeed, today I know far better what it means to be the Lord's bride under the sign of the Cross. But since it is a mystery, it can never be understood by reason alone".... Gradually, throughout her life, as she grew in the knowledge of God, worshiping him in spirit and truth, she experienced ever more clearly her specific vocation to ascend the Cross with Christ, to embrace it with serenity and trust, to love it by following in the footsteps of her beloved Spouse*

The third example is much simpler, but it brings out a beautiful aspect of vicarious suffering. It involved the English writer, C.S. Lewis. He was standing by the bedside of his wife, Joy, who was dying of cancer. She was in terrible agony. Lewis asked God if he could experience some of his wife's pain. His prayer was answered when he felt a horrible pain in his legs which lasted for several minutes. At the same time he saw a look of relief and peace come over Joy's face. This exchange was made possible not only by faith, but more importantly because of Lewis' deep love for his wife. It was another form of vicarious suffering.

A fourth example played in Molokai, Hawaii. The Belgian priest Damien de Veuster asked his bishop to go to Molokai to care for the lepers there. He told his bishop, "I know many of these unfortunate souls and I ask only to share their lot and their prison." And a prison it was—a prison of degradation, suffering, and death. Damien set out to restore the dignity of these lepers. He organized them into work groups that constructed roads, cottages, and clinics. He organized footraces, even for those who had lost their feet. He cheered the island by forming a choir and a band. Two organists who had ten fingers between them played at funeral Masses.

Damien's Christian wisdom directs us on our path in life:

> *The memory of your past infidelities must move you at each present moment to acts of humility and contrition, with the renewing of firm vows for the future. Be severe towards yourself, indulgent toward others.*

Our fifth example is probably much closer to home. It is about Fr. Solanus Casey, a Capuchin priest canonized in 2018. When Father Solanus died in Detroit in 1957, all he left after 86 years on this earth were a small crucifix, an old pair of sandals, several religious pictures, a wooden statue of St. Anthony, some dog-eared religious books, a knot of heavily darned socks, and a framed, 40-year-old picture of his family. It says in one of his biographies, "He saw... that the only cure for mankind's crime and wretchedness was the love that can be learned only from and through Him who died to show men what love is."

Two times he was rejected for what his dream was: becoming a priest. The first time he was dismissed from a diocesan seminary because of his poor academic performance. The second time, he barely made it through the Capuchin seminary. Since he ranked only in the lower part of his seminary class, his teachers recommended that his priestly office be severely restricted to a "simplex" priest. He could say Mass but was not permitted to preach from the pulpit; he was not allowed to hear confessions. So he ended up tending the door as a doorkeeper. He could have echoed what the other saintly doorkeeper, Brother André Bessette, used to say, "My superiors showed me the door, and I stayed there forty years." Fr. Solanus never complained, but offered all the disappointments of his life up to God for the sake of others. He used to say, "If we want to rise with Christ we must be ready to die with Christ."

Fr. Solanus' humility never allowed him to feel embarrassed when a sinner asked him to hear a confession and he had to call for another priest to be the confessor. He simply accepted, like his Master had, what God had allowed for him. That was his hidden cross that he carried without saying a word. In exchange for his sacrifices, Jesus gave him power to heal others—a power that was literally miraculous. During his years as doorkeeper, he filled seven notebooks with more than 6,000 requests for help from petitioners. And to some 700 of these he reported cures from cancer, leukemia, tuberculosis, diphtheria, arthritis, blindness, and other maladies. Fr. Solanus ranks among the most prodigious wonder-workers in Church history. Without his suffering, none of those miracles could probably have happened.

Our sixth example may seem rather exceptional, but probably happens much more than you realize. It is about Élisabeth Leseur (1866–1914). During her life she was hardly known outside her social group of cultured, educated, and generally antireligious friends. She was married to Félix Leseur, a medical doctor and well known as the editor of an anti-clerical, atheistic newspaper in Paris. The attacks of her husband against Christianity and religion prompted her to probe deeper into her faith. At the age of thirty-two, she thus underwent a religious conversion. From this time on, she saw her major task in praying for the conversion of her husband, while remaining patient with his constant attacks on her faith. She loved her husband too much to allow their home to degenerate into an emotional war zone. She realized that confrontations and arguments were useless; she chose instead to pray for Felix and keep quiet, without saying a word.

In 1899, she began keeping a secret diary, in which she recorded how she used his efforts to destroy her faith as means to grow in love for him and for God. She also used her physical pains to pray for her husband. Because she had had hepatitis as a child, the disease recurred throughout her life with attacks of increasing severity. She offered to God all the little difficulties, the annoyances, as well as the more painful trials of illness. In one of her notes, she thanked Felix:

> *Thank you for everything, and above all else, for being you. And forgive me for being me, that is to say, someone who by herself is not worth much, and who is a bit improved only under the influence of suffering she has accepted, and accepted only through a help and a strength greater than my own. Because of this, you must be indulgent with the convictions that time and God have made deep, and thanks to which I have not become bitter and selfish.*

She wrote in her diary, "Not one of our tears, not one of our prayers is lost, and they have a force that too many do not suspect." And force they had! After her painful death, Felix found her notebooks that she had concealed for so long to keep the peace at home. He was deeply touched by her diary, and finally realized she had quietly offered years of great suffering for his conversion. After that experience, Felix not only embraced Christ, but also became a Dominican priest who traveled throughout Europe speaking about his wife's spiritual writings. When Archbishop Fulton Sheen made a retreat under the direction of this Fr. Leseur, he learned of the life of Elisabeth and the conversion of Félix. Sheen subsequently repeated this conversion story in many of his presentations.

Our seventh example is probably much more widely known: Pope John Paul II. We all witnessed how he suffered dramatically from Parkinson's Disease at the end of his pontificate, which not only affected his movements but also his speech. Cardinal Stanislaw Dziwisz, a long-time and influential aide to and friend of Pope John Paul II, said about his ailing friend,

> *Today there is a cult of beauty and strength, of youth, but he showed that suffering has a redemptive value to humans and also for society. Indeed, the Pope wanted to suffer for the Church and for humanity, as all the saints have done.*

These examples could be expanded with many, many more. There is a long line of exemplary Christians who showed us that no one can save us except the crucified Jesus. And if we want to save others, we have to join the crucified Christ. In the writings of the Saints, we find an astonishing reality, telling us that it is precisely suffering that strengthens us, humbles us, and forges us into saints, so we become like St. Paul: "I have been crucified with Christ; it is no longer I who live, but Christ who lives in me; and the life I now live in the flesh I live by faith in the Son of God, who loved me and gave himself for me" (Gal. 2:20). Ironically, it is in the midst of our suffering, without saying a word, that most of our growth and maturation takes place. The fact that most Saints happen to be physically and/or spiritually broken can hardly be a coincidence.

Of course, you don't have to be a Saint to share in Jesus' suffering—but you may become one. It is not only very saintly people who suffer vicariously—that is, for the sake of others. Pope Benedict XVI encouraged all of us to follow their example:

> *As Jesus confronted the evil one with the force of love that came to him from the Father, so we too can confront and win out in the trial of sickness, keeping our hearts immersed in God's love.*

What can we learn from all the examples above? Our wounds can become a source of healing, not only for ourselves but also for others. That's how we become "wounded healers." Just as no one can be led out of the desert by someone who has never been there, no one can heal brokenness who has not been broken himself.

This way, our suffering becomes a *sacrifice* for the benefit of others. In modern-day vocabulary, "sacrifice" is a scandalous word that we try to avoid at all times. We like to blurb it out. We live in a world that runs away from suffering. Since the time of our youth, we have been conditioned to view suffering as an impediment to happiness. We look for ways to end the pain rather than ways to embrace it. Even a simple headache can send us hurrying to the medicine cabinet for a speedy cure. This worldview, which is so embedded in our modern culture, tells us that the less we suffer, the happier we will be.

How different is Christianity! In Christian vocabulary, "sacrifice" is a glorious word. The scandal of the cross, as St. Paul calls it, translates into the scandal of sacrifice. There is something mysterious about it—which is the core message of Christianity. Nabeel Qureshi, who converted from Islam to Christianity could not have said it better: "To be a Christian means suffering real pain for the sake of God. Not as a Muslim would suffer for God because Allah so commands him by fiat, but as the heartfelt expression of a grateful child whose God first suffered for him."

Suffering is an intrinsic part of our lives since the Fall in Paradise. There is an energy in suffering and a power in the cross that we can only experience by letting our own suffering become part of Jesus' suffering. Pope John Paul II put this in his own words:

> *Many of our contemporaries would like to silence the Cross. But nothing is more eloquent than the Cross when silenced! The true message of suffering is a lesson of love. Love makes suffering fruitful and suffering deepens love.*

After all the beautiful words said about suffering and brokenness so far, you may wonder whether I am glorifying suffering here. I don't think so! But it may seem so, especially for people who live in a world that runs away from suffering. Since the time of our youth, we have been conditioned to view suffering as an impediment to happiness. Yet we could be missing out on another dimension of suffering, for suffering has the mysterious potential of redeeming us, transforming us, transfiguring us. Suffering can be very therapeutic. Whereas Stoics say "Suffering is nothing," Christians say "Suffering is everything." In all that happens to us, even in suffering, we can participate in Jesus' suffering that had redeeming power. Some people said to Mother Teresa, they wouldn't do her work for a million dollars. She quipped she wouldn't either, but she would do it for God.

The Cross of Golgotha calls for a dual approach—it's both a sign of suffering and a sign of healing. It's like with pain. On the one hand, pain is a sign of suffering, of something that is going wrong in our bodies. On the other hand, pain is also a sign of growth—like when the first teeth break through. As Alcoholic Anonymous says, "No pain, no gain." God does not miraculously remove our problems, but he shares them with us, as he did on the Cross of Golgotha. So now we can share our problems with him. To whom else can we bring all our pain if not to Jesus on the Cross? As Archbishop Fulton Sheen put it, "Do not feel that suffering is an obstacle on the road to heaven; it can be the road itself."

The ancient Church used to sing, "God reigns from the wood of the Cross." In other words, suffering is not meant to make us bitter, but *better*. To the left of Jesus's Cross was someone who felt bitter, to the right someone who felt better. We have a choice as to which one we want to be—the better one or the bitter one!

7. The Journey Home

Where Is Home?

The journey "home," after death, is not a journey to a place where we had been before. "Home" is the place where we were meant to be from the very beginning: Paradise—a place that Adam and Eve, including all their descendants, were driven away from. It is a place we never really knew, just like Monarch butterflies fly to a place they have never seen before, and yet they know where to go, following some kind of built-in compass. They go to a place where their ancestors came from, but unknown to themselves.

We, human beings, also know where to go when we die—it's the place our first ancestors came from. However, that doesn't mean we have automatic access to the Paradise from which our first ancestors were removed. Being descendants of Adam and Eve does not entitle us to a guaranteed entrance. Not only did Heaven have to be re-opened for us by Jesus' Crucifixion, but we also had to gain our original birth rights back again.

Each time I attend a funeral, I marvel at how easily the deceased person is promoted and elevated to Heaven. Our culture, dominated by the slogan "me, myself, and I," tends to believe that God *owes* us a place in Heaven. One time, a troublemaker asked Archbishop Fulton Sheen a question about someone who had died. The Bishop replied, "I will ask him when I get to heaven." The guy replied, "What if he isn't in Heaven?" The Bishop replied, "Well, then you ask him." His response made clear we do not automatically end up in Heaven to meet everyone we had known before.

Yet, if we go by obituaries and funeral speeches, all of us seem to end up in Heaven. How comforting to hear! According to gravestones and prayer cards for the deceased, we all seem to automatically "rest in peace" after death. If the deceased had incorrigible habits of sin, well, let's not make them feel uncomfortable by publicly condemning the sins they were prone to; and let's tell them that God is merciful, forgiving, and tolerant, and that we are not the final judges. Let's also remind them that all sins can be instantaneously wiped away in the confessional or on a good deathbed—or even without that. Above all, let's tell them that you don't have to get an A-plus in sanctity, a D-minus will do just fine. So the bottom line is that we are all supposed to go "back home" where we really belong and deserve to be.

How true can this be? I sincerely wonder, for this sounds to me more like one of those advertisements trying to sell us snake oil—something that promises everyone much more than what it can deliver: a perfect product, without any faults or side-effects, for a low discount price. We should know better. There is this joke of a man who had done awful things in life, but when he died, his brother promised the pastor a generous financial kickback if he would mention in his eulogy that the deceased man had actually been a saint. The pastor promised he would do so in exchange for the kickback. So when the time of the eulogy came, he gave a short and very honest biography of the deceased, and then ended with the words, "But compared to his brother, he was a saint."

Somehow, we are all declared saints at the moment we die, no matter how we had lived our lives. However, the hard truth is that we will in fact be *judged*. We will not be judged by our feelings but by our deeds—that is, by our virtues and vices, our good deeds and our sins. As we said earlier, because God is not only a God of Mercy but also a God of Justice, there will be a final judgement for each one of us. We all leave life with a broken soul, but some souls are more stained than others. It's up to God to judge how serious our remaining stains are. In the words of the Catechism (1039, 1040):

> *In the presence of Christ, who is Truth itself, the truth of each man's relationship with God will be laid bare. The Last Judgment will reveal even to its furthest consequences the good each person has done or failed to do during his earthly life.*
>
> *The Last Judgment will reveal that God's justice triumphs over all the injustices committed by his creatures and that God's love is stronger than death.*

Fortunately, we are not judged by other people, but by God. Human beings are not good or fair in judging themselves or others. Therefore, we will be in for many surprises when we find out that the ones we expected to be in Heaven are not there, and the ones we did not expect to find in Heaven turn out to be there.

"Home" is good news and bad news. It is bad news for those who have too many serious stains to be forgiven. The best we can do is hope and pray that God may forgive us. We can't repeat the last sentence of a *Hail Mary* often enough, "Pray for us sinners, now and in the hour of our death." However, there is also good news. The good news is that "home" is a place where all our tears will be wiped away—tears from broken souls, broken hearts, broken families, broken generations, and a broken world. As the Book of Revelation (21:4) puts it: "He will wipe every tear from their eyes, and there shall be no more death or mourning, wailing or pain, [for] the old order has passed away."

This doesn't mean, though, that Heaven is a place only for people who never had tears and sufferings. There is this story of a person who had suffered much and had entered a Heaven where he found no one who had been broken in life. Not surprisingly, this person could never feel "at home" there. Heaven is not a place for people who have never sinned, neither is it a place for people who were never broken. There is no space in Heaven for people without scars. As Saint Rosa of Lima said so pointedly, "Apart from the cross, there is no other ladder by which we may get to Heaven." Even Jesus, after his Resurrection, still carried the scars of his Crucifixion (John 20:15).

Most of us are very familiar with the parable of the two sons. It can be found in Matthew 21:28-32. It is the story of a man with two sons who told them to go work in the vineyard. The first son refused, but later obeyed and went. The second son initially expressed obedience, but actually disobeyed and refused to work in the vineyard. The son who ultimately did the will of his father was the first son because he eventually obeyed his father's wish. Jesus then likens the first son to tax collectors and prostitutes—the outcasts of Jewish society—because they believed John the Baptist and accepted "the way of righteousness" (21:32), in spite of their initial disobedience to the Law.

But some have suggested there should have been at least a third son in the story—the son who left home and never came back. Authors such as André Gide (in his book *The*

Return of the Prodigal Son) and Harold Pinter (in his play *The Homecoming*) have proposed this third possibility. It does make sense. It is the reality of life. We all know fallen-away Catholics who never came back to their Catholic Faith before they died, not even at their death bed. They could make for the third son who left home and never came back.

Did Jesus forget that third son, that third possibility? It's hard to believe. He knew there are only two possibilities: you stay with the Father, or you walk away from him but come back later. There is no way you can stay away forever. The Father's house is the place we belong. Eventually, we will all have to face the Father—either burdened with resentment or relieved with repentance. We all go ultimately back to the Father. But whether he will let us enter his eternal home, Heaven, is an entirely different question. We could end up in the "pigs' stable" of the Father's House. In other words, that third son never existed. The third possibility is in essence never a real option for us.

Most of us want to be welcomed back home. People have a natural yearning to be waited for and welcomed back, both in this life and in the life to come. People can keep their sanity as long as there is at least one person who is waiting for them. And the good news is: that one person is God in the end. But it certainly helps when other people are there for you, too, both before, during, and after you die. This always reminds me of the legendary Monsignor Hugh O'Flaherty, who was immortalized in the well-known movie *The Scarlet and the Black*. The movie tells the story of how O'Flaherty and his friends concealed 4,000 escapees, mainly Allied soldiers and Jews, in flats, farms, and convents. When Herbert Kappler, the head of the *Gestapo* in Rome, learned of O'Flaherty's actions, he ordered a white line painted on the pavement at the opening of St. Peter's Square—signifying the border between Vatican City and Italy—stating that the priest would be killed if he crossed it.

Thanks to O'Flaherty's organization, thousands of escapees were saved. When the Allies liberated Rome in June 1944, 6,425 of the escapees were still alive and had escaped Kappler's brutal actions. Ironically enough, Kappler himself had to eventually call on the very O'Flaherty he had hoped to kill, so as to organize a safe exit for his wife and two children during the liberation of Rome. O'Flaherty followed his conscience and obliged! But Kappler himself stayed behind and was arrested by the Allies and sentenced to prison for life. This is where this real story had an unexpected twist. O'Flaherty regularly visited his old archenemy Herbert Kappler in prison, month after month, year after year, being Kappler's only visitor! Fifteen years later, in 1959, Kappler converted to Catholicism and was baptized by O'Flaherty, who had been waiting for him to call him back home. The rest of the story is in God's hands, of course.

The Way Back Home

What could the way-back-home look like? Did we ever personally experience anything like it? I would be surprised if anyone has any memory of how we came into this world at birth. But, based on biology and psychology, we do have an idea of what this experience must have been like. When we were born, we were "expelled" from the dark womb into a world unknown to us. Even when there are no complications at the time of birth, various dramatic changes have to take place for every baby at the moment of birth. The placental circulation has to be cut off; the temporary connection between the pulmonary artery and the aorta needs to be closed; any temporary openings in the wall between the left and right heart ventricle and between the left and right atrium have to be closed; the lungs will be inflated for the first time; and blood will be forced into the pulmonary circulation system. We all have gone through this process successfully, and hopefully unharmed. We were never asked whether we wanted to be born—we just had to surrender to this transition. That's how we entered our "home" here on earth.

Well, something similar may be happening when we are being pushed through the "birth canal of death" leaving behind the comforting world to which we had become so accustomed. The transition from this life to the next stage through the process we call biological death—from home-on-earth to home-in-Heaven—is often painful and frightening in a similar way. We all fear the prospect of death, as it is saying farewell to all that was dear to us, as well as to all that was not so dear to us. Woody Allen, of all people, once joked he wasn't afraid of death but didn't want to be around when it happens.

If the analogies between birth and death hold true, however, we should not be so fearful, for just as this life surpassed existence within the womb, so too could the next life surpass all we have experienced here on earth—with "hands" waiting to receive us at the other end. A life after death only makes sense in terms of life before it. Nobody can envision a new earth when there is no old earth to hold new promises for us.

Who would choose to remain unborn after having experienced even some of the riches of life? Something similar may hold for embarking on a journey beyond death. As a matter of fact, we have no choice but to embark on this journey beyond death. We may feel like Monarch butterflies who "know" when to migrate to a land they have never been to, along a route they have never followed before. In a similar way, the human soul also "knows" there is a time to "migrate" to where its eternal "home" is. It returns to a place it has never been to before. Yet, we were born with an innate desire to look beyond: to the grass on the other side of the mountain, to the land on the other side of the ocean, to the stars beyond the stars we can see—and also, which is much more important, to life on the other side of death.

Are there any indications that there is indeed a way through the tunnel of death? The centuries-old Catholic answer is that there is such a way: when the soul leaves the body after death. Is there any proof that this is possible? It's indeed almost literally a million-dollar question. When James Kidd of Phoenix, AZ, was found missing and presumed dead in 1949, he had left a last will and testament, offering about a half-million dollars—the equivalent of six million in 2018 dollars—to anyone who would do research to offer concrete proof that the soul leaves the body after death.

Amazingly, such research has been done since. In 1975, Raymond Moody, a medical doctor, published *Life after Life*, a book on "near-death experiences" of patients who had been resuscitated after clinical death, many of whom had extraordinary experiences of separating from the body and eventually returning back to life. And that book was just the beginning. His book has been followed by a multitude of books and articles documenting thousands of cases in which resuscitated individuals reported viewing procedures in operating rooms, passed through walls, saw relatives and friends in waiting rooms, followed a tunnel toward a bright light radiating love and compassion, often met deceased loved ones along the way, and either were sent back, or chose to return, to their bodies. These are the phenomena that are usually reported after an individual has been pronounced clinically dead or was otherwise very close to death—hence the term *near-death-experience* (or NDE). Those who have had such experiences usually swear by them and remain utterly convinced that there is a dimension of a person that survives physical death.

According to a recent Gallup poll, approximately eight million Americans claim to have had a near-death-experience; however, the exact number of people who had near-death-experiences may be much higher because people who had this experience may not feel comfortable discussing what they experienced with others, especially not when such an experience is often understood as a paranormal, or even weird, incident.

Probably the most extensive, ground-breaking clinical study of NDE was done by Pim van Lommel, a cardiologist in the Netherlands. With his team, he studied a group of Dutch patients who had been brain-dead from cardiac arrest but were successfully revived. Of the 344 patients who were successfully resuscitated after suffering cardiac arrest, 62 had experienced "classic" NDEs, which included out-of-body experiences. Of these 62 patients, 50% reported an awareness or sense of being dead, 24% said that they had had an out-of-body experience, 31% recalled moving through a tunnel, whilst 32% described meeting with deceased people. None of those patients reported a distressing or frightening NDE. The patients remembered amazing details of their conditions during their cardiac arrest despite being clinically dead with a flat EEG of brain stem activity.

The cardiologist Van Lommel assumed that his findings supported the theory that consciousness had continued despite lack of neuronal activity in the brain—with a flat EEG, that is. Van Lommel comes to a powerful conclusion:

> *Our most striking finding was that Near-Death Experiences do not have a physical or medical root. After all, 100 percent of the patients suffered a shortage of oxygen, 100 percent were given morphine-like medications, 100 percent were victims of severe stress, so those are plainly not the reasons why 18 per cent had Near-Death Experiences and 82 percent didn't. If they had been triggered by any one of those things, everyone would have had Near-Death Experiences.*

What is even more remarkable is that Melvin Morse, M.D., a specialist in pediatrics, found similar results among young children. That's so amazing because most children have never heard or even had the occasion to hear about near-death-experiences, nor are they motivated by personal, cultural, or religious beliefs. Morse compared his study group of 12 children, who were resuscitated from cardiac arrest or who had returned from deep comas, with a control group of 121 children who were severely ill but not resuscitated or in deep coma, and an additional control group of 37 children who had received large doses of mind-altering drugs but were also not resuscitated or in deep coma. He found that none of the 121 children in the control group experienced anything like a near-death-experience. In the study group, on the other hand, 8 out of 12 had near-death-experiences.

Striking in all NDE cases is the accuracy with which NDE patients report their experiences. In the Dutch study, one man who had been in a deep coma, later told a nurse that he recognized her and saw where she had placed his dentures during resuscitation efforts, and even described the cart into which she had placed them. Similarly, Melvin Morse reports that a woman had knowledge of a shoe on a window ledge outside the hospital (not near the room where the patient was resuscitated, but next to a fifth-floor office where she was being interviewed). The psychologist who did the interview had to crawl along the ledge outside her window to verify the claim and to find the shoe indeed there. Some patients even reported leaving the operating room and visit their relatives and friends in hospital waiting rooms. One patient reported seeing her young daughter wearing mismatched plaids. Another woman overheard her brother-in-law talking to a business associate in the hospital waiting room in a very derogatory manner, and was able to report this back to him later.

Though it is truly significant that patients with normal eyesight are able to report with great accuracy sensorial data that occurred while they were unconscious, it is even more significant that *blind* patients are able to do the very same thing with the same degree of accuracy. Kenneth Ring, Ph.D., and his coworkers studied 31 blind patients of whom 14 were blind from birth and evidently had no experience of seeing. They found that 21 of them had a near-death-experience and 10 of them had out-of-body experiences only. The fact that they were accurately reporting what they could not have seen with their physical bodies gives a high degree of credibility to a non-physical existence during a near-death-experience. Kenneth Ring summarizes his findings as follows: "80 percent of our thirty-one blind respondents claimed to be able to see during their NDEs.... [They] often told us that they could see objects and persons in the physical world, as well as features of otherworldly settings."

Do these findings have anything to do with life-after-death? Fr. Robert Spitzer, S.J. has studied these reports but is very careful in his assessment of such NDE phenomena, for this is dangerous territory, hiding potentially explosive landmines.

Yet, he concludes that these findings "suggest strongly that human consciousness, perception, memory and movement survive bodily death... and in many cases the surviving persons are led to a loving and heavenly domain." Is it not very likely, Fr. Spitzer speculates, that these experiences demonstrate the existence of a trans-physical dimension to the self? They are hard to explain by any other hypothesis. So he feels entitled to conclude, "We have evidence that human beings survive bodily death, that we have a soul that literally leaves the body." Then he elaborates:

> *The corroborated veridical sensorial knowledge by both sighted and blind patients is very significant because there does not appear to be any physical explanation for these corroborated phenomena, leading to the conclusion that there must be some form of nonphysical conscious existence (including self-consciousness, memory, intelligence, and self-identity), and some survival of nonphysical embodiment (which allows for interaction with the physical world).*

What do these NDE findings prove? Probably not much in the technical sense. It is certainly not a scientific proof for eternal life, if only for the fact that there is no guarantee this nonphysical survival of consciousness and sensation will last forever. Besides, although these are impressive cases, with all being "near death," none of the people who had a near-death-experience actually *died*—they came back. Yet, these findings do indicate that NDE phenomena are hard, if not impossible, to explain in purely bodily terms—for the brain is just not working during a flat EEG.

No wonder, NDE is often cited as evidence for the existence of the human soul, the after-life, and perhaps even heaven and hell—concepts well known from some religious traditions. Many individuals who experience an NDE do see it as a verification of the existence of an after-life—including those with agnostic or atheist inclinations before the experience. In her memoir, *To Heaven and Back: A Doctor's Extraordinary Account of Her Death, Heaven, Angels and Life Again*, spinal surgeon Mary C. Neal, M.D., explains how, in her own NDE, she was drowning in a kayak, until God told her she still had other work to do.

Of course, people with a critical or skeptical mind have the right, or even the duty, to question such conclusions. Not surprisingly, all kinds of *biological* explanations have been suggested instead: oxygen deprivation (anoxia), high carbon-monoxide levels, REM-sleep phenomena, psychedelic agents, hallucination. However, the question remains why not all people under those circumstances had ND-experiences. Besides, more research has been done to rule these explanations out. A study by Dr. Sam Parnia suggests that NDE patients are "effectively dead," having no neural activities necessary for dreaming or hallucination. Additionally, in order to rule out the possibility that near-death-experiences resulted from lack of oxygen, Parnia rigorously monitored the concentrations thereof in the patients' blood, and found that none of those who underwent the experiences had low levels of oxygen. He was also able to rule out claims that unusual combinations of drugs were to blame because the resuscitation procedure was the same in every case, regardless of whether they had a near-death-experience or not.

Besides, the question remains of how such biological explanations can even begin to explain the fact that those who have "exited" their bodies can describe their environments with such remarkable accuracy. And how can these theories possibly explain how people, blind from birth, correctly see objects and colors in the environs of the sites where they died?

Perhaps we may cautiously assume that ND-experiences do offer us a peek through the "birth canal" of death—some kind of window into the after-life. Death may not be a final destination, but there may very well be a better purpose awaiting us. Arguably, this is not hard evidence in a scientific sense, but as they say, absence of evidence does not imply evidence of absence. We should keep in mind that most neuroscientists would not allow for any non-material explanations anyway. A fair response to this controversy would be to not let hard-core proponents of materialistic explanations talk away anything that cannot be counted, measured, or quantified—including life after death. Let us keep in mind that there is a real problem for those who say that physical death is the only *certainty* there is. If "physical stuff" is all that counts, then all our certainties are on their way out as well. For if I am certain that everything is physical, I would have no reason to suppose that this certainty is true—and hence I would have no reason to be certain that everything is physical, and physical only.

Van Lommel poses the million-dollar question: "How could a clear consciousness outside one's body be experienced at the moment that the brain no longer functions during a period of clinical death with flat EEG?" Perhaps the best and safest answer is that there is something more here than a physical body—the non-physical soul that is. This may answer the question whether humans have a soul that can exist after bodily death. What these near-death-experiences do suggest is that the soul—and its intellectual part, the mind—can survive brain-death. These findings seem to at least confirm that there can be mental activities without neural activities associated with a flat-EEG.

If this is true—and there is not much reason to doubt it is—then not only is death a necessary part of life, it could also be a necessary *stage* in life—a stage of transition into another kind of life perhaps, not an ending but a transformation. Seen in this light, what we call the last stage may very well turn out to be the next-to-last stage, when seen in a wider than biological context. As shown earlier, when we came into this world, we went already through a rather similar transition by leaving the protective shelter of our mother's womb. At that moment, rather abruptly, life in the womb was over. It must have been a shocking, almost traumatic, experience when we were pushed out of her womb, had to go through the tunnel of her birth canal, and were forced to breathe on our own—a physical and emotional shock, for sure. At that moment, we were certainly entering a very different and unknown world. We had to trust that we could live there and that there were hands welcoming us. We were fortunate to find out that there was life beyond life in the womb.

Unfortunately, we have to add that some did not find "hands" welcoming them outside the mother's womb. They had the experience at birth that their father, or even their mother, had forsaken them—which creates a lifelong brokenness of heart. Broken families create broken hearts. But, fortunately, God has taken on this brokenness. For even if there were no hands waiting for us at birth, there will be "hands" waiting for us at death. As Psalm 27:10 tells us: "Even if my father and mother forsake me, the Lord will take me in." And in Isaiah (49:15-16), God touches our broken hearts:

> *Can a mother forget her infant, be without tenderness for the child of her womb? Even should she forget, I will never forget you. See,*

upon the palms of my hands I have engraved you.

But the fact remains that, when you die, you leave behind "life"—your own life. If death is really and truly death, you are destroyed forever—never again to be "you," never again to think or to feel, never again to laugh or to love. But if there is something beyond biological death, then there must be another dimension of life that we may have overlooked or misunderstood—an immaterial dimension not limited by space and time. True, if we are just biological machines, we certainly die—and that's it. But if we are more than biological machines—bodies formed by souls, including mind and will—then biological death may not be the end.

If the near-death-experiences we have been discussing here are real—and indications are they are—then there may be a larger purpose looming in life, changing our lives into a purpose-driven life, reaching even beyond death. If the purposes we had in previous stages of life were real, why could the last purpose we have in life not be real, too? If someone asks me, "Are we alone in this universe?" my answer would be, we are not! I am not stating here that there must also be other forms of life in this universe—perhaps there are. But even if there are, we would still be alone... unless there is a God.

Let's close this section with a quote from the Catechism (1060):

At the end of time, the Kingdom of God will come in its fullness. Then the just will reign with Christ forever, glorified in body and soul, and the material universe itself will be transformed. God will then be "all in all" (1 Cor 15:28), in eternal life.

What Is Heaven Like?

Is there a Heaven? If there is life after death, then there must be a Heaven: if there is no heaven, then there is no hell; if there is no hell, then there is no sin; if there is no sin, then there is no judgment, and if there is no judgment then evil is as good as good is evil. If, however, we do accept there is good and evil, then there must somehow be a Heaven where good is rewarded and evil punished. If Heaven is indeed our final, eternal destination, it is very understandable that we would like to know what Heaven is like. No one has come back to earth to tell us, for being in Heaven means not being on earth anymore. Let's not forget that the revelations some Saints had about the after-life were mostly not of Heaven, or even Hell, but rather of Purgatory.

How can we ever capture something from Heaven while we are still on earth? St. Paul gives us a glimpse of the answer: "At present we see indistinctly, as in a mirror, but then face to face. At present I know partially; then I shall know fully, as I am fully known" (1 Cor. 13,12). We all know here on earth that we are finite beings with a finite mind—if you don't, think again. But somehow our human mind, finite as it is, is able to catch a glimpse of the Infinite. To use a poor analogy: If I can count from one to ten, or from one to thousand, then I can also count from one to infinity, at least in theory. Somehow, we have the inborn capacity to reach out to infinity.

Applied to ourselves, the human mind has the capacity to reach beyond itself. This capacity is rightly called self-transcendence—referring to the transcendence of something, or rather someone, more than our own selves. We can even say about ourselves, "I am only human"—thus comparing ourselves, not with something "below" us (such as a cat, a dog, or an ape), but with something, or rather Someone, "above" us and transcending us. I cannot transcend myself on my own, of course, but because I myself was made in the image of God, I perceive more than myself whenever I perceive myself more completely. We see something similar in our everyday experience of imperfections in justice, love, goodness, and beauty—which indicates an innate sense of perfection that brings us to apprehend the possibility of encountering perfect justice, perfect love, etc. The only place where this can really come true is in Heaven.

Most people have a rather primitive, childlike idea about Heaven. The Muslim heaven, for, instance, is a man's haven where each man is rewarded with seventy-two beautiful, high-bosomed virgins, plentiful food, slaves galore to attend to every whim and wish. Apparently, the bliss there comes from base sensual pleasures—food, drink, and sex. Even in the eyes of some Christians, their own Christian heaven is not much different. They portray heaven as a place of eternal picnics and "lions laying down with lambs." But we shouldn't forget that lions, lambs, and picnics get boring after a while. Or they picture heaven as an endless repetition of alleluias or the monotonous fingering of harps. Even that can get boring! Or they "eternalize" what they liked doing on earth—playing piano, puttering in the garden, and so on—but there are no pianos and gardens in Heaven. No wonder, Cardinal Ratzinger warned us in one of his books against depicting Heaven as an extension of this life prettied up with idyllic depictions. That easily makes for "Bumper Sticker Christianity."

If that's not it, what then is Heaven really like? To put it in a nutshell, the bliss of Heaven comes from the pure joy of being in God's presence. It is more a *state* of being than a *place* somewhere in the clouds. As the Catechism (2794) says about the line "Our Father who art in heaven" at the beginning of the *Our Father*,

> *This biblical expression does not mean a place ("space"), but a way of being; it does not mean that God is distant, but majestic. Our Father is not "elsewhere": he transcends everything we can conceive of his holiness. It is precisely because he is thrice holy that he is so close to the humble and contrite heart.*

As Hell is a state of eternal damnation, Heaven is a state of eternal salvation. The language of "place" is, according to Pope John Paul II, inadequate to describe the realities involved since it is tied to the temporal order in which this world and we exist. Although the Book of Revelation does provide a physical description of heaven—the New Jerusalem with walls of jasper, gates of pearls, and streets of gold—we must be mindful that such imagery conveys the inexpressible, incomprehensible beauty of Heaven rather than intends to be a literal description. God does not occupy some remote geographic corner of the physical universe, and no MapQuest search can tell us exactly where Heaven is. It is a "state" rather than a "place."

So, a "state" then? That may not sound as much, but it is actually everything we could ever dream of. We will see God face to face, not with physical eye balls but with the spiritual "eyes" of the soul. Our physical eyes fail here—St. Paul actually warns us not even to try to conjecture what Heaven will be like, "No eye has seen, nor ear heard, nor the heart of man conceived, what God has prepared for those who love Him" (1 Cor. 2:9). As St. John puts it, "we shall be like him, for we shall see him as he is" (John 3:2). No matter how broken we were on earth, we will also see at last how our brokenness was used by God. Besides, "He will wipe every tear from their eyes, and there shall be no more death or mourning, wailing or pain, [for] the old order has passed away" (Rev. 21:4). That means no sickness or any imperfection will be possible in Heaven. This is much more than you might think: In Heaven, questions we've always had will be answered. And so much more, according to the Catechism (2040):

> *We shall know the ultimate meaning of the whole work of creation and of the entire economy of salvation and understand the marvelous ways by which [God's] Providence led everything toward its final end.*

As Pope John Paul II pointed out on July 28, 1999:

> *In the context of Revelation, we know that the "heaven" or "happiness" in which we will find ourselves is neither an abstraction nor a physical place in the clouds, but a living, personal relationship with the Holy Trinity. It is our meeting with the Father which takes place in the risen Christ through the communion of the Holy Spirit.*

This is often called "beatific vision." In the 4th century, St. Ambrose explained what that is:

> *How great will your glory and happiness be, to be allowed to see God, to be honored with sharing the joy of salvation and eternal light with Christ your Lord and God,... to delight in the joy of immortality in the Kingdom of heaven with the righteous and God's friends.*

Archbishop Fulton Sheen worded this as follows,

> *Heaven is not a place where there is the mere vocal repetition of alleluias or the monotonous fingering of harps. Heaven is a place where we*

> *find the fullness of all the fine things we enjoy on this earth. Heaven is a place where we find in its plentitude those things which slake the thirst of hearts, satisfy the hunger of starving minds, and give rest to unrequited love. Heaven is the communion with perfect Life, perfect Truth, and perfect Love.*

In short, Heaven is our ultimate destiny, back home, where all our brokenness can be healed and all our tears can be wiped away. Despite humanity's inability to save itself from its brokenness, God is the one who heals a broken world in Heaven. In the words of the Catechism (1024), "Heaven is the ultimate end and fulfillment of the deepest human longings, the state of supreme, definitive happiness." True and everlasting happiness can only be possible with God. At the moment we meet God face to face for the first time, we will have something that is a million times more spectacular than any relationship we had on earth.

How does one enter Heaven? As we said before, to come to God and be saved, you need to repent, have faith and hope. No one's saved who doesn't want to be. Archbishop Fulton Sheen once said, "Had Christ remained on earth, sight would have taken the place of faith. In heaven, there will be no faith because His followers will see; there will be no hope, because they will possess; but there will be love for love endureth forever!" Although in Heaven there will be no faith, since faith is of things unseen, nor hope, since hope is of things not yet possessed, Heaven is our ultimate hope while we are still on earth. The Catechism (1818) says about hope:

> *The virtue of hope responds to the aspiration to happiness which God has placed in the heart of every man; it takes up the hopes that inspire men's activities and purifies them so as to order them to the Kingdom of heaven; it keeps man*

> *from discouragement; it sustains him during times of abandonment; it opens up his heart in expectation of eternal beatitude.*

Obviously, if it were true that there is no God and no Heaven, then there would be no hope for this broken world—with its broken souls, hearts, families, and generations. This broken world needs hope. So let us end with what St. Teresa of Ávila says about hope:

> *Hope, O my soul, hope. You know neither the day nor the hour. Watch carefully, for everything passes quickly, even though your impatience makes doubtful what is certain, and turns a very short time into a long one. Dream that the more you struggle, the more you prove the love that you bear your God, and the more you will rejoice one day with your Beloved, in a happiness and rapture that can never end.*

Endorsements

"The causes and the cures of the brokenness and unhappiness in our broken, unhappy world are obviously many and complex, but in *Broken Hearts in a Broken World,* Gerard Verschuuren reduces the complexity to clarity and then prescribes with great good sense. This is a wise and provocative book that deserves to be read widely and put into effect everywhere."

— Russell Shaw, Consultor of the Pontifical Council for Social Communications, adjunct professor at the Pontifical University of the Holy Cross in Rome, former Secretary for Public Affairs of the National Conference of Catholic Bishops/US Catholic Conference.

"Verschuuren's book *Broken Hearts in a Broken World* is a wonderful treatise, full of fresh insights. Using philosophy to refute skepticism and relativism, Verschuuren also provides a panoramic view of all that gives us hope in our Christian vision. There is no cliché advice, but instead blunt, witty, realistic and compassionate analysis of the ills of our times and the wounds in our hearts."

– Ronda Chervin, Professor Emerita, Holy Apostles College & Seminary, Cromwell, CT

Index

About the Author

Gerard M. Verschuuren is a human biologist, specialized in human genetics. He also earned a doctorate in the philosophy of science. He studied and worked at universities in Europe and the United States. Currently semi-retired, he spends most of his time as a writer, speaker, and consultant on the interface of science and religion, faith and reason.

Some of his most recent books are:

- *God and Evolution?—Science Meets Faith*. (Boston, MA: Pauline Books, 2012).
- *The Destiny of the Universe—In Pursuit of the Great Unknown*. (St. Paul, MN: Paragon House, 2014).
- *Five Anti-Catholic Myths—Slavery, Crusades, Inquisition, Galileo, Holocaust*. (Kettering, OH: Angelico Press, 2015).
- *Life's Journey—A Guide from Conception to Growing Up, Growing Old, and Natural Death*. (Kettering, OH: Angelico Press, 2016).
- *Aquinas and Modern Science—A New Synthesis of Faith and Reason*. (Kettering, OH: Angelico Press, 2016).
- *Faith and Reason—The Cradle of Truth*. (St. Louis, MO: En Route Books, 2017).
- *The Myth of an Anti-Science Church—Galileo, Darwin, Teilhard, Hawking, Dawkins*. (Kettering, OH: Angelico Press, 2018).
- *The First Christians—Keeping the Faith in Times of Trouble*. (St. Louis, MO: En Route Books, 2018).
- *The Eclipse of God—Is Religion on the Way out?* (St. Louis, MO: En Route Books, 2018).

- *Forty Anti-Catholic Lies*. (Manchester, NH: Sophia Institute Press, 2018.
- *The Destructive Doctrines of Our Age*. (St. Louis, MO: En Route Books, 2019).

For more info:

http://en.wikipedia.org/wiki/Gerard_Verschuuren.

He can be contacted at www.where-do-we-come-from.com.

www.ingramcontent.com/pod-product-compliance
Lightning Source LLC
Chambersburg PA
CBHW032225080426
42735CB00008B/719
* 9 7 8 1 9 5 0 1 0 8 0 1 5 *